'Towards the Oxford Street end stands  enterprises of the book world – Foyles By sheer genius they made it the busie known to me. One may go at any departments – and there seems no end to them – and find everywhere a packed concentration of students seeking books and advice. The atmosphere is that of a great, preoccupied busy-ness; the assistants are inexhaustible encyclopedias; whole ranges of cheap classics, new school books, histories, dictionaries, novels, and in fact everything, as far as everything can now be obtained, is at hand for the student's need. There is, of course, a rare book department in Foyles, where those more exclusive in taste can rove; but for the most part this is a store for men and women of small means in search of essential tools.

As an institution it is overwhelming.'

Frank Swinnerton, *The Bookman's London*, 1951

Foyles
a celebration

Penny Mountain

with Christopher Foyle

BOOKS

First published in 2003 by Foyles Books

A CIP catalogue record for this book is available from the British Library

ISBN 0 9544952 0 9

Designed and Typeset by Ned Hoste/2h
Typeset in Bembo
Printed and bound in Great Britain by
BAS Printers Ltd, Stockbridge, Hants

Foyles Books
An imprint of
W & G Foyle Ltd
113-119 Charing Cross Road
London WC2H 0EB

www.foyles.co.uk

Contents

Introduction

It is one hundred years since brothers William and Gilbert Foyle embarked on an enterprise that was to become "The World's Greatest Bookshop". This year also sees Foyles hold its 700th in the series of Literary Luncheons conceived by William's daughter Christina. This book is not intended to be an official history of Foyles, although there is an historical element in it. Rather it is an affectionate, anecdotal, sometimes candid celebration of a bookselling institution that has survived the vicissitudes of the twentieth century to emerge with renewed vigour in the twenty-first.

Foyles has played an important part in the lives of those who have worked in it, shopped in it and written books that sell in it. The bookshop has earned itself a worldwide reputation in bookselling and a reputation for eccentricity, not least because of its rather unusual retailing practices – the inspiration for many a good story but now thankfully in the past. *Foyles: A Celebration* aims to reflect this quirkiness, to pick out some of the highlights of the first one hundred years and to celebrate, often in their own words, both the vitality of its founders and the people behind the scenes and behind the tills who have made Foyles famous.

Christopher Foyle

March 2003

CHAPTER 1

THE STORY OF FOYLES

A man bought a book from a bookseller. He took it back because of some scribbling on the title page. The scribbling was by Ben Jonson. Worth hundreds! [William]

In 1906, three years after setting up in business, William and Gilbert Foyle took a lease on 135 Charing Cross Road

The Beginnings

I often think what a wonderful time they must have had. My mother and father only 19 and 20 and my Uncle Gilbert, 19, with the bookshop. [Christina]

William and Gilbert in 1903

One hundred years ago, two teenage brothers, William and Gilbert Foyle, failed their Civil Service examinations. They decided to sell their textbooks, and advertised them. Such was the response that they could have sold them many times over, so they determined to start a bookshop. The unwanted textbooks became the modest foundation stone of what was to become the world's greatest bookshop.

William's vision was a bookshop for the people – not just for academics, collectors, specialists or the gentry but for every man, woman and child, of any station in life: 'The People's Bookshop'. He was inspired by James Lackington's Temple of the Muses at Chiswell Street in London in the late eighteenth century, whose galleried bookshop was so large that, it was said, a coach and six could drive around inside it. William was an authority on the lives of booksellers of the past, and he modelled himself on Thomas Guy and James Lackington. Guy had made his fortune in bookselling and publishing, and used it to found Guy's Hospital, while Lackington had once owned London's biggest bookshop. William even had a soft spot for the 'unspeakable' Edmund Curll, who, during the eighteenth century, produced books of 'an indecent character', according to the *Cambridge History of English and American Literature*.

The two brothers' business expanded so rapidly that within thirty years their shop was internationally famous, holding a stock of five million volumes on thirty miles of bookshelves, making the name of Foyles synonymous with bookselling the world over. The shop that exists today is still unrivalled for its range and depth of stock.

William and Gilbert, the seventh and eighth children of William Henry Foyle, were born in Shoreditch, London, in 1885 and 1886 respectively. In 1843 their grandfather, George,

UNUSUAL REQUESTS, FULFILLED BY WILLIAM:

For the "best book published for £500": supplied the Kelmscott *Chaucer*

For the "worst book published for £500": supplied complete set of Marquis de Sade illustrated

had migrated to Hoxton from Portsmouth, where he had been chief butler at Government House to General Sir Thomas McMahon. He came to London to seek his fortune with his wholesale dry-salting – to preserve fish and meat – and grocery business. During the Napoleonic Wars George's father, Thomas, had moved from an agricultural life in Bower Chalke, a small village near Salisbury, to make ships-of-the-line for Nelson's navy in Portsmouth dockyard. His family can be traced back to 1374 in the village of Fontmell Magna in Dorset.

Both William and Gilbert won scholarships to Owen's School in Islington (now Dame Alice Owen's School in Potters Bar) and from there to King's College, London University. Here they studied for another three years, intending afterwards to enter the Civil Service. When that plan failed, they were forced to consider other possibilities.

William took a post with the eminent KC Sir Edward Marshall Hall, who collected old

The Foyles van in 1917, a regular in the London area collecting second-hand books for resale

silver and took to sending his young clerk to the salerooms on his behalf. However, books had always been William's passion, and on those occasions he would bid for any that caught his attention. It was soon evident that a career in law would not suit him: not only did his interests lie elsewhere, he was partially deaf and had difficulty in following court proceedings.

Meanwhile, Gilbert had become a clerk with Shoreditch Borough Council, for whom he took charge of public baths and wash-houses, and the banking of the takings. It was tedious drudgery for which he earned a pound a week. At the end of a year he asked for an extra shilling a week, which was refused.

The brothers were ready for change, even though perhaps they had not realised it. And, of course, they needed money.

The response to their textbook advertisement was such that William and Gilbert purchased more books to sell, this time through primitive hand-written catalogues as well as advertisements. They based themselves and their stock in their parents' kitchen in Fairbank Street, Hoxton. As the business grew, they took over the dining room, and eventually moved into disused premises in Islington at a rent of five shillings a week. This was soon followed by their first 'shop', a lock-up in Peckham. Their tenancy had to be negotiated by post: the pair were still only seventeen and eighteen and their evident youth would have put paid to an agreement. Gilbert left his job with the council to run it, but William continued with Sir Edward Marshall Hall and helped his brother in the evenings. Their turnover in their first year of trading was £10.

From the outset, William and Gilbert were confident that their business would be a success, and despite the difficulties they faced while they were establishing it, their conviction did not waver. They cooked their meals at the back of the shop over an oil stove – sausage and mash was their staple diet. They had no leisure time – no half-days, no free evenings or Sundays: they worked from seven in the morning until midnight every day.

They soon discovered that speedy service brought recommendations and more business, so they set up a system to ensure that customer

I consider Charing Cross Road the worst architecturally and morally in the world, but it has a wonderful fascination. At night one sees every type of person and every nationality strolling along. It was the site of our shop that Dickens chose as the background to A Tale of Two Cities. *Soho round the corner has two characters: innocent by day, villainous by night. Houses that look respectable by day open their doors at night to the most sinister interiors. People one meets there lead double lives. [William]*

orders were delivered as quickly as possible. Each morning's orders were examined as soon as they arrived, and the new or second-hand volumes in stock were parcelled up and taken by William on his bicycle to the City. Here, after his office hours, he found the rest of the books he needed to fulfil the orders, and despatched them all from the Post Office before he returned to the shop. The business was flourishing when Sir Edward dismissed William – for, as William admitted, 'incompetence' – so he was not put out. He recalled that one counsel in the chambers had called him a 'bloody fool', and 'Years after he was our counsel in a case which he lost, and so I reciprocated the expression.'

In 1904 the brothers took a significant decision to leave the suburbs in favour of central London. They found a site in Cecil Court, a small but busy pedestrian link between Charing Cross Road and St Martin's Lane, in an area already occupied by other booksellers. The rent of the shop was sixty pounds a year, considerably more than they had been paying

Foyles leads the way in low-priced books and late night trading – an early marketing initiative

in Peckham, which meant they had to broaden their customer base. They expanded their stock from Civil Service and other textbooks to a selection of general books. 'We made up our minds to try to supply Every Book Required,' said William. But it was hard work. 'At Peckham, we bought about 100 bound volumes of *Graphic*. They weighed about a ton – moved them on a barrow with Gilbert in the shafts and myself in the rear. Barrow tipped up on the tramlines. Volley of oaths and curses!'

Soon they had engaged an assistant – a mistake: he absconded with the day's takings of seven pounds, a considerable sum at this time, so the partners had to husband their resources even more carefully. Lunch usually consisted of bread, cheese and ginger beer. Return of the empty bottles raised enough for part of the tram ride home to Fairbank Street; otherwise they walked. In later years, Gilbert became a keen rambler. But the problem of an assistant remained.

In 1905 Tom Gale was passing through Cecil Court and saw two young men in their shirtsleeves carry out a small bookshelf and a few armfuls of books – the 'outside stock' of the shop. What prompted him to approach them will never be known, but they took him on at six shillings a week. He remained with the company until his retirement in the 1950s.

By early 1906 the bookshop's postbags were bringing in so much business that the police paid the brothers a visit, suspecting an illegal lottery or other shady dealings. Later that year William and Gilbert had to move again, but they felt justified in taking a fourteen-year lease on larger premises at 135 Charing Cross Road, as well as the Cecil Court shop and other outlets at 1 Cambridge Avenue, Kilburn, and 65 Grand Parade, Harringay. Soon after they opened branches in Shepherds Bush and Brixton. They had been in business for only three years, but were already describing themselves as 'The Largest Educational Booksellers in London'. Accountancy and law books were a speciality and another department was dedicated to medical texts. On 3 July 1919

A Charing Cross bookseller called to see some books at Streatham. All were rubbish except a first edition of Lamb's Tales worth £150. His offer for the collection was refused, so he asked the dear old lady if he could choose and read a book on the bus home. He said he was very fond of Lamb's Tales. 'Yes, my good man. Have it with pleasure!' [William]

W. & G. Foyle was incorporated as a limited company with an authorised share capital of £16,000.

They bought books wherever they found them: in salerooms, from students, other individuals and second-hand bookshops. One shop William visited was in New Oxford Street, run by a Christina Tulloch, a descendant of seafarers from the Shetland Islands. She thought he was a poverty-stricken student and let him have books cheaply. In 1907 they were married. Their first child, Winifred, was born in

1909, followed by Christina in 1911, then Richard in 1912.

The business continued to grow and the brothers were soon employing nearly a hundred assistants and purchasing books by the thousand. Yet another move became necessary and this time the brothers did not hesitate: in 1912, they moved to a six-floor building on the corner of Manette Street and Charing Cross Road, across the road from the present shop. Now they could stock books on a wide variety of subjects – art, theology, music, education, naval and military, occult and psychic, agriculture, technical, rare books, first editions and much more. The extra space also offered better scope for the control of books, and they developed a new system of classification and category sections.

In 1912 the Foyles also began to trade in new books – the first publisher to give them credit was Heinemann – but their main business was still in second-hand. In 1922 they claimed to have over a million volumes in stock, and by 1929 they were buying an average of 40,000 books each week and employing 140

Brother Gilbert had an idea of flower-boxes frontside Charing Cross Road shop. But when the dirty water trickled down the necks of people looking at the books we gave it up. [William]

staff, who included two to help with the buying. The 'outside buyer', Bradley of Foyles, as he was known, covered London and a radius of fifty miles round the city. He travelled an average of five hundred miles a week and made a hundred calls; the collecting van brought his purchases back to Charing Cross Road. The 'indoor buyer' sorted through the unwanted books of countless households and libraries, which were sent to the shop in paper parcels, boxes, sacks and old travelling trunks from dusty attics: the past favourites of students, readers and book-collectors, which would either find a new home or be pulped by the waste-paper merchants. Among many valuable purchases Foyles made were six copies of the limited second edition of *The Seven Pillars of Wisdom*, which each fetched in the region of £500, an immense sum in the late 1920s. Later, when the book was reprinted at thirty shillings, Foyles ordered seven thousand copies from the publishers. It was a record order in the history of bookselling, but astute buying was an essential function of the business. More stock was acquired from publishers, at book auctions, from bankruptcies, country-house clearances, and from people who brought their books direct to the buying department. When Bernard Shaw decided to dispose of his surplus books when he moved from his spiked-railed fastness in the Adelphi, he turned to Foyles. It was one of the most successful deals that, until then, the firm had negotiated.

The impetus behind this was William Foyle: he lived for and dreamed about books. He went to endless trouble to track down unusual or rare books, and from the start Foyles earned a reputation for supplying books on even the most out-of-the-way subjects.

The business was still growing and space, again, was at a premium. The Foyles bought Dickensian premises in Manette Street from the Reverend Basil Bourchier, then vicar of St Anne's, Soho. In 1929, the Lord Mayor of London, Sir J. E. Kynaston Studd, opened Trefoile House, a splendid new five-storey building on the site of the Old Goldbeater's House, mentioned by Dickens in *A Tale of Two*

William Foyle, co-founder of W. & G. Foyle Ltd

Living in Archway Road, Highgate. Police station opposite. At 3 a.m. one morning there was a knock. Police asked: 'Are you the manager of Foyles?' I said yes. He said, 'The place is on fire.' I said, 'Let it burn – I am not walking in to town at this hour.' He said, 'If I were Foyle I would give you the sack.' [William]

Christina Foyle, William Foyle's daughter, founder of the Literary Luncheons and successor in the bookshop business

Cities. This, although Foyles' finances were a perennial problem: 'No money at all,' William recorded. 'We could hardly pay salaries, yet signed the lease of new premises for £1250 a year! Worked day and night to get it in order, and opened with enormous banner across the road and colossal press notices. It was packed every day and queues of people.'

The banner brought its own problem: its slogan, 'The Largest Bookshop in the World Just Opened', proved a source of irritation to the local authorities. After a month, Foyles received urgent demands to take it down, but ignored them. The authorities approached the Sun Electric Company across the street, who threatened to cut the end suspended from their building. Later that day a gale blew up and tore the offending banner in half.

Foyles' postbag was now averaging more than two thousand letters a day, and in the busy seasons, at the start of academic terms, more than five thousand, from every part of the world, reached through advertisements in

THE STORY OF FOYLES

*A very wealthy KG started collecting books.
He bought first editions in original cloth, stripped the
covers and rebound the whole of his library in scarlet
morocco. A complete set of Scotts worth about £1000
reduced in value to £100 . . . [William]*

papers and journals that circulated in homes
from the grandest to the lowliest. The firm was
also issuing 150,000 catalogues each year.

One of the more famous advertising stunts
for which the Foyle brothers were responsible
was selling books by weight – at twopence a
pound. This unusual method of book retailing
created widespread publicity in Britain and
America: one offended trade journal described
the practice as 'trading better suited to
greengrocery'. The Foyle brothers would
probably have agreed – and smiled: their
scheme brought in yet more business, not only
from passers-by but from bargain seekers all
over Britain.

Foyles encouraged clubs and societies to visit
the bookshop, no doubt with an eye to
building its customer base. But the company
was also a generous benefactor, forever sending
books as gifts to charities, hospitals, schools,
churches and missions.

*Another typical day [in 1912]:
Dr Duncan had a fit
Miss Bishop left
Miss Hatton, bilious attack
Miss Tulloch, sick
Mr Hobbs gave notice
A man ran amok:
killed 1 person, injured 3
[William]*

Monday a very bad day. Everything gone wrong. Staff giving notice; complaints etc. Called to see a friend at Chigwell, Essex, chauffeur lost his way in Blackout. Ran over a dog and a cat; got in a cul-de-sac. Arrived very late. Lady greeted me at the door. I stood on a mat on a slippery floor, went flat on my back. Arrived home late, wife very cross, thought I would drown my sorrows in a drink. Saw a bottle of port on sideboard, took a big swill. It was turpentine. Well, I said to myself, call it a day! [William]

Branching Out

The 1920s and 1930s at Foyles were decades of frenetic growth and experimentation. Not every new idea had legs, but it always had panache.

In 1921 Foyles Educational was launched, under Gilbert's direction, after the brothers had purchased a small educational-contracts firm. It supplied textbooks and prizes to schools all over the country, and also issued *The Coronation Book of King George VI*, of which nearly a million copies were sold – another record that Foyles had set.

Meanwhile, the Library Department supplied public libraries the length and breadth of Britain. In its heyday in the 1960s and 1970s, under Aird Thomson, it was a considerable business, employing four representatives and about two dozen back-office staff who processed and serviced the library orders. In the main the operation supplied town and county public libraries, visited by the representatives, although the librarians themselves often came to the shop to select stock. Library supply being a labour-intensive business, the department contributed significant turnover to the company but little to the bottom line and it was closed down in the 1980s.

In the 1920s when the Welsh population in London was said to number around 200,000,

Brother gave an uplift talk to girls at an approved school. Felt he had done a good job. Found his car all scribbled with vulgar remarks and all tyres flat! [William]

and there were thirty-six churches and about sixty literary societies in which the proceedings were conducted in the language, Foyles Welsh Company was established at 16 Manette Street. In 1927 Foyles Welsh Press was founded to publish some of the most important Welsh books. Its first title was *Caniadau'r Allt*, a book of Welsh lyrics by Eifion Wyn; the first edition of three thousand copies sold out in four weeks. In 1928 Foyles procured a van to travel in Wales

Staying at Tintagel, Cornwall, for holiday. Went bathing, can't swim, caught by the tide and went under three times. Clutched hold of Christina's hair. All my wicked past went through my brain. Son Dick on shore thought I was playing a usual joke. Strong lady swimmer rescued me and I lost consciousness. Swallowed gallons of water. [William]

distributing Welsh books from door to door.

Also in the 1920s Foyles Music Company opened, carrying a stock of over a hundred thousand gramophone records and a large number of second-hand gramophones, and Literary Lectures were held in the bookshop on Wednesday evenings. There, enraptured audiences listened to speakers such as the Sitwells, Arthur Conan Doyle and Walter de la Mare. In June 1927, the firm launched a magazine, *Foylibra*. It offered staff with writing aspirations the opportunity to shine in print, and kept customers up to date with what was going on: new staff, promotions, marriages, visitors, author news, book news, exhibitions, films of books, obituaries, news of the owners' comings and goings, comments from customers. It was bound round a literary magazine, latterly *Books and Bookmen*, and survived until autumn 2000. It remains a rich and entertaining archive.

In January 1930, the Reverend Basil Bourchier was on hand to perform the opening ceremony at the Foyles Art Gallery, whose motto was 'Art for all'. It aimed to provide a venue for seeing and buying works of merit by the 'coming men' – and women, as it turned out. Over the years the displays have been numerous and varied, from ceramics, embroidery, Chinese painting and wallpaper to 'Art by Nurses' and 'Soho Photographs'.

Nineteen thirty also saw 'a most novel development in the history of the House of Foyle': Foyle's Educational Films. It was set up to advise on, develop, print, produce and distribute films of every kind – scientific, educational and 'propagandist' – outside mainstream entertainment. There was even a private theatre so that customers could project their own films for their friends.

James Laver [curator at the Victoria and Albert museum] wanted to write a book on underclothes, but his wife would not let him. Willett Cunnington wrote a very comprehensive book on the subject, which was published at about five guineas. We sold hundreds of copies – nearly all to clergymen. [William]

In 1934 Foyles initiated and developed Foyles Libraries Ltd, a chain of three thousand 'twopenny libraries' that aimed to place 'good, sound' fiction within the reach of a constantly increasing reading public. With its outlets in every large town in Britain, as well as in Ireland, India, Palestine, Australia, South Africa, Egypt and even a number of ocean-going liners, it afforded the general public the opportunity to read for only twopence a book. Until then library subscriptions had been expensive, so available only to the monied classes. At any one time nearly three quarters of a million volumes were out on loan. By the late 1930s Foyles was also running the Piena Music Company, specialising in musical instruments and accessories.

Among the most important of Foyles' innovations were the book clubs. In 1937, Foyles launched the Right Book Club – legend has it that it was a counterbalance to Victor Gollancz's Left Book Club. By the 1940s it had diversified into several clubs, each covering a different subject: the Book Club (New Fiction), Children's, Scientific, Garden, Quality,

Pet aversion: Board and Committee Meetings. We seldom have any, and son and daughter and myself decide on transactions running into thousands within a few minutes. [William]

Religious, Classic, Women's, Thriller, Western, Catholic, Travel and Romance. Also by then Foyles had opened branches in Dublin, Belfast, Johannesburg and Cape Town.

In 1944 Foyles took over the Lecture Agency, originally founded in America by Civil War veteran G. W. Appleton, which provided a sparkling list of top-flight speakers to address luncheon clubs and other groups all over Britain.

At the trial of Crippen we were able to produce in court an American medical book describing the drug hyacinthine, which helped in the prosecution. We bought up the library of Armstrong, who was hanged for murdering his wife. The library contained every book on poisons. [William]

I was in Rome when Mussolini was in power – Il Duce on all the hoardings. Went into a café, ordered wine and stupidly shouted, 'Viva Mussolini.' Knives were drawn and I ran for my life. It was a den of Communism. [William]

Artist's impression of **Foyles, Charing Cross Road,** used on the front cover of *Foylibra* from the 1950s to the 1980s

In 1952 the agency hosted a lunch at the Dorchester for the secretaries of nearly 100 women's luncheon clubs, to discuss planning for the coming season, which resulted in an enormous number of bookings. Over the years the speakers included authors, explorers, broadcasters, politicians and many others – Gilbert Harding, Lord Birkenhead, Sir Adrian Boult, Sir Arthur Bryant, Vera Brittain, Lady Violet Bonham-Carter, Godfrey Winn, Tony Benn, Baroness Ewart Biggs, John Timpson, Edna Healey, Leslie Thomas, Norman Croucher, Phil Drabble, James Herriot, Sir Ranulph Fiennes, Godfrey Talbot, Lady Rothnie and Sir Chris Bonington.

The agency has now closed, but on taking over the bookshop in 1999, Christopher Foyle and Bill Samuel discovered that its elderly manager, Kay Whalley, was still running the almost defunct business. The sole interest of her adult life had been Foyles, retirement was out of the question, so she continued on the payroll until her death a year later. She had loved the company, was highly regarded by the many famous speakers on the agency's books, liked and respected by Foyles staff, but, reportedly, never saw eye to eye with William's daughter, Christina.

In 1949 William Foyle founded his eponymous Poetry Prize presented every year for the most outstanding volume of poetry. It was discontinued in 1963 after his death, but in 2002 the Foyle Foundation resuscitated it in the form of sponsorship of the Foyle Young Poets of the Year Award, which is run by the Poetry Society.

By the 1950s Foyles was also publishing books, which included a large range of Foyle Handbooks, initiated by William, on how to breed and care for popular varieties of dog and other animals, as well as books on gardening and antiques collecting published under the John Gifford imprint. For many years the firm ran a special department servicing the book requirements of students enrolled with a number of correspondence colleges.

No stone was left unturned. When Foyles realised that its sacks of post from overseas offered a golden opportunity, it created a

Lord Justice Darling was in the shop. He offered me 4/- for a book marked 7/-. I said, 'My Lord, if you sentenced me to 7 years in your court and I suggested 4 years, would you agree?' Eventually he gave me 5/-. [William]

Processing book club orders in 1951

FACTS AND FIGURES

In 1925:

- Foyles employed 94 assistants.

- 22 different catalogues were issued yearly.

- Of one catalogue alone (School Books) 50,000 copies were printed.

- A day's post averaged 2000 letters.

- 1900 customers were served in one day.

- The stock consisted of more than 1.25 million volumes on 22 miles of shelving.

- 800,000 volumes were sold annually.

- There were 18 departments:

Library	Topographical
Educational	Fine Art
Scientific	Naval and Military
Technical	Economics
Medical	Rare Books
Theological	Foreign Books
Occult	Remainder
Law and Commercial	Oriental
Music and Drama	Sport

Generally wear a bowler. Would visit a local hostelry frequented by well-known boisterous footballers. Of course they pinch the hat and play football with it. Next day a new one awaits me. [William]

A sell-out: *Lady Chatterley's Lover*, after publication of the unexpurgated text by Penguin in 1960

Philately Department to sell the foreign stamps 'at bargain prices'.

The Foyles Entertainment Department was another 1950s initiative. It was set up with a view to providing entertainers for parties, bazaars and other functions – toastmasters, compères, dance bands, film-shows, puppets and marionettes. Sadly, there is no record of how

Volunteered for the crowd scene in Julius Caesar *at the Old Vic during the war. I could not keep the toga on so used a lace from a sandal. As I walked off stage I left sandal behind. Christina, aged six, yells out, 'Look, Mummy, there's Dada.' [William]*

Shopping at Foyles

the enterprise fared. At some point a Foyles Handicrafts Shop was opened, offering a selection of tools and materials for, among others, basketry, leather- and raffia-work, artificial flower-making and marquetry. In the 1960s Foyles even offered a Travel Bureau. Its sun-and-snow programme included fifteen days in Kitzbuhel, by air, for £55 10s. – a snip, today, at £750.

In 1954 the firm's turnover was £2 million, but by 1963 it had doubled – worth around £80 million today.

In 1966 the rebuilding of the south side of Manette Street (started in 1929 with the construction of Trefoile House) was completed with the opening of Goldbeater's House, a fine new seven-storey block providing four floors for the bookshop and three floors of apartments.

Throughout Foyles' history there has been a strong link between the family and the bookshop. William's son Richard, known as Dick, worked in the business until the outbreak of the Second World War when he joined the Navy. After he was invalided out he returned to the shop as its buyer, remaining in his post until he died suddenly in 1957 at the tragically early age of forty-five. Christina and Dick's sister Winifred worked in the Music Department

Dusting some of the twenty-two miles of shelves in 1955

Seldom broke a promise even when hard up.
Seldom forgot a request.
Seldom late.
[William, of himself]

from 1928 until her marriage in 1937, and her husband Edgar Samuel, a colourful character, started and ran the book clubs until he joined up during the war. Unusually today, Foyles is still a family-owned business. Two of William Foyle's grandsons – Christopher Foyle and Bill Samuel – are board directors, and run the shop.

Christopher joined Foyles on the shop floor in December 1961. The following year he went abroad for a period of apprenticeship in bookselling and publishing, first in Stuttgart, then Berlin. He returned to London briefly for Foyles' glittering sixtieth anniversary dinner and his twenty-first birthday, then set off for Finland and Paris. By 1972 he found that his hopes of any real responsibility in managing the business

Artist's impression of
Foyles, Manette Street, in
the 1990s

The Pope joined the Catholic Book Club, but payments were made under another name. We sued him unwittingly [presumably for an overlooked invoice]. Only people who ever sued the Pope. [William] were increasingly elusive – he was full of ideas for improvements but unable to implement them. 'It was quite an emotional wrench,' he remembered. 'Until then, I had no ambition other than to work in and ultimately run the family business.' He went on to set up his own successful air-cargo business, which he continues to run.

Six days before her death on 8 June 1999 Christina made Christopher a director of Foyles, and he was appointed managing director and chairman of the company on 6 September 1999, retrospectively from June 1999. His cousin Bill, a chartered accountant and former investment banker, joined him on the board later that year.

Filling the bath with water the tap jammed and I could not turn it off. I shouted to wife to help. The bath was near to overflowing. 'Why don't you take the plug out, silly?' [William]

William's children: from left, Winifred, Richard (Dick) and Christina

William Alfred Foyle

*Had very severe
nasal catarrh.
Left gas on under
the geyser in the
bathroom. When
lit, it blew up,
almost blew me
out of the
window, but
cured the catarrh.
[William]*

A family outing to Broadstairs in 1955. From left: Nanny
Sylvia, Dick's wife Alice, with their son Anthony on her lap,
William (seated), Winifred's daughter Margaret, Dick and
Alice's son Christopher Foyle, Winifred (seated), Winifred's
youngest daughter Julia, Winifred's oldest daughter Christina
(seated), Dick (seated), Mrs William Foyle (Christina Tulloch,
seated); Winifred's son Bill Samuel is taking the photograph

In 1945, William retired

from active management of the business to
enjoy life in the country and his unique
antiquarian library. During the 1930s, he had
kept a sailing boat at Fambridge, near Maldon,
and had come across Beeleigh Abbey, a twelfth-
century, Premonstratensian monastery, while
walking in the area. He had fallen in love with
it, and spent nearly a decade trying to persuade
its elderly owner to sell it to him. He
succeeded in 1944. When he and his wife
moved in, there was no gas, electricity or mains
water.

The business was now in the hands of his
daughter Christina and her husband Ronald
Batty, but William continued to take a keen
interest and travelled up to London every
Friday. Each weekday a large bag containing
customers' letters and invoices was despatched
to him at the Abbey and he would spend the
day reading through them, then send

Beverley Nichols mentions wild book trade parties soon after 1st War. Went to one in a flat over a sweetstuff shop in Clerkenwell. Well-known actors etc there. We went out to buy drinks and saw a huge dummy Guinness bottle in a grocer's window. We persuaded him to sell it to us for 2/6d. We took it back and filled it with beer. When lifted up the bottom collapsed and the beer went through the ceiling to the shop. Police were called but he joined in the party. [William]

instructions and advice to the staff who had handled them.

He got up at five thirty each morning, and spent his leisure hours leafing through his fabulous collection of books – medieval manuscripts, Books of Hours, hand-written and illuminated on vellum by monks, and his first, second, third and fourth folio Shakespeares – playing croquet or bowls in the garden or with his Bassett-Lowke steam and electric 0 gauge model railway in the attic.

That is, when he was not playing practical jokes on his guests. Once, apparently, he decided to clean out the Beeleigh goldfish pond, on the site of the monks' burial ground. When he had emptied it, he discovered it was full of human bones. The dustmen refused to take them away, so, when visitors were going round the Abbey, William would slip out and fill the boots of their cars with them.

Undoubtedly WF, as he was known in the book trade and by all his employees, was one of the greatest booksellers of all time. His genius lay in his ability to place his hand upon the exact book a customer wanted. A member of his staff wrote: 'This gift has probably worked more advantages for the firm than any other; it might be said that William Foyle is a greater bookfinder than a bookseller.' It was common at busy times to see a shirtsleeved William delving 'with the energy of a mole

When hard up and wanted new blinds, put a box by cash desk 'For the Blind'. [William]

through wet clay' through piles of recent purchases in search of a rare book.

William set much store by his having been the seventh child of a seventh child, and reckoned he had second sight: 'Saw a book *Story of an African Farm* and had an intuition that someone important would call and ask for it. Put it on the windowsill in my office. The Prime Minister of New Zealand called with a publisher and asked for it. Was astounded!' And: 'Arranged to fly from Brindisi, Italy, to Athens, but had a premonition something would happen and cancelled. The plane was wrecked and several people killed.'

On the book-buying front there were numerous 'lucky finds': a first edition of Omar Khayyám, purchased for twopence in Caledonian Market, sold for £2000; an Isle of Wight clearance revealed a first folio Shakespeare; Dr Samuel Johnson's boyhood prayer book; a fourth folio Shakespeare; a first edition of Thomas Hardy's *Dynasts*; and the remainder copies of Edgar Wallace's first novel,

Brothers-in-law and fathers of the current directors: Edgar Samuel and Dick Foyle at Christina's marriage to Ronald Batty, on 30 January 1938

Four Just Men – 1500 copies at twopence each, 'now buying back at £90 a copy!'.

Sometimes things didn't go William's way. Having purchased Baroness Burdett Coutts's library he sold a parcel of books to another bookseller for five pounds without looking at them. Among them was a rare Shelley pamphlet, which the other bookseller sold for £2000. He never let William forget it: 'Got any more Shelley pamphlets?' he would ask, whenever they met.

More often than not, though, William was canny. During the 1930s many antiquarian-book dealers operated a bidding cartel, which William refused to join. Once when he arrived for a sale in Hampshire, he found that his competitors had taken the only cab at the station. Undaunted he hitched a ride in a hearse, got there before the others and bought several lots. They wanted to know how he had stolen such a march on them and, when he told them, were outraged: 'We even took our hats off as you passed.'

William Foyle, bidding at an auction in 1954

According to Christina, it was not until the late 1940s that Foyles started to make money. Until then, all profits had been ploughed back into the business, air raids discouraged shopping and the bookshop owed 'thousands'. Thanks to the support of publishers, particularly Macmillan, Hodder and Heinemann, Foyles survived. In addition, paper rationing meant that fewer new books were published, and the value of old ones soared. At the end of the war many collections of books came on the market as families sought to realise their assets, and the enterprises that had been set up between the wars at last began to flourish.

The trials of managing the great business seemed not to ruffle William, yet the bookshop's precarious finances weighed on him. He found an answer to that, though: 'Would get fed up with worry, work and creditors,' he records, 'so took Tube to Hampstead Heath. Brisk walk for hour and half. Returned very refreshed.'

He had a talent for turning his memories of difficulties to humorous account. On one occasion – 'Very hard up and lots of bills due' – when Gilbert was running Foyles Educational and was in credit, William asked his brother to lend him £500 to meet a bill. Certainly not, Gilbert replied, exhorted William to pay his own way, and returned to dictating a letter. William remembered that his brother was fond of the word 'semi-colon'. When Gilbert hesitated to consider his next sentence, William broke in: 'Semi-colon, Gilbert.'

'Ah, good, yes, that's right! Well, what do you want, Will?'

'Five hundred pounds,' came the reply.

'Make it a thousand to tide you over.' A cheque was made out on the spot.

Another story concerns William's long-suffering bank manager, who summoned him one Saturday morning to account for an overdraft: 'I said, By the way, Charlie, it's my birthday today. "Oh," he says, "we must celebrate." So we adjourn to Long's Famous Wine Bar, Hanover Place, and have several sherries. He says, "Now what would you like?" I said, I am rather short of boiled evening shirts with collars to match. Taxi to Austin Reeds.

Bought a number of autographed letters of Bernard Shaw from a well-known journalist. Sold to American for £150. Turned out to be forgeries (forger got 6 months). Wrote to B. Shaw and asked our legal position. He wrote back about four pages. We refunded the £150 and sold the forgeries (as forgeries) with B. Shaw letter for £200. [William]

I said, Chuck in two bows. He replies sarcastically, "I suppose you don't want a top hat [10 guineas] and an evening cloak". No, I say, I think that will be enough. So kind of you, Charlie, and so forth. We part, "Happy Birthday" etc.

'Monday morning, furious rings on the phone. "Is that you, William? What the hell have you been up to? I see in my diary your birthday was 4 March, when I gave you a bottle of whisky." Oh, I says, Saturday last was my *spiritual* birthday, the day I was baptised. "Well, don't do it again. Goodbye." Bangs down receiver. I took him to a big swell dinner hoping he could swell the overdraft. Had opposite effect and he cut it down.'

Christina, whom William called Babs, could also be put to good use: 'My father had discovered that creditors were kinder to me than they were to him, so he did not throw himself into the struggle against bankruptcy, he threw me into it.'

William loved dogs, especially large ones. When he was first married, he had a magnificent St Bernard called Wallace, who travelled with him to business on the Tube. The dog knew where to get out. Once as a woman stepped over him, Wallace got up and carried her the length of the carriage. He was followed by Pasha, a bad-tempered Borzoi who detested publishers' representatives and never missed an opportunity to growl at them.

Christina adored her father – 'his exotic good looks, his magnificent head, dark brown eyes, and curling black hair'. Although of average height, William had great presence, excellent sartorial taste, beautiful hands ('because he never used them') and great exuberance. In every photograph, he appears

with his long hair curling on his collar and a grin on his face. Beneath the joviality, though, 'he had a brilliant and subtle mind'.

He frequently offered Christina a thousand pounds: as a schoolgirl, to translate a play by Molière, later to organise Foyles' Literary Luncheons, or if she would keep on an ancient retainer at Beeleigh (or the same sum if she hastened his departure). She never saw the money: 'Somehow you could never pin him down.'

From time to time he turned up to join in with his children's games: 'He was like a

Was chatting with Dennis Wheatley [the well-known writer, originally a wine merchant]. Wine was then in very short supply. I said, 'Can you get any sherry?' He said, 'Not much; as a matter of fact my cellar is very low just now. I have only about 6 dozen sherry, 8 dozen ports and 6 dozen champagnes left.' As my cellar consisted of about 3 of each I thought I had better shut up. [William]

delightful elder brother with his jokes and leg-pullings and fun,' Christina said. 'He always seemed so much younger than other people's fathers and he never behaved like them.' William noted that because he perpetually worked late he hardly ever saw his children: 'One of them wanted to know who the man was who came in on Sundays.'

While other children went to the Zoo, the Foyle children and grandchildren visited the bookshop, where they met the many distinguished people, eccentrics, authors and Bohemian characters of the Charing Cross Road area, whom William attracted with his vitality and humour: the amazingly good-looking Compton Mackenzie; the wicked Aleister Crowley; Conan Doyle, with his embroidered satin waistcoats; Laurie Wright, the music publisher, reputed to have had six wives; and Willie Clarkson, the wig-maker of Wardour Street, with his falsetto voice and red curls.

William's grandson, Bill Samuel, remembers him as a wonderful grandfather: 'He gave us a love of books and mischief in equal measure,

Never tasted breast of a chicken, always the leg. When I was young, the parents had the breast, and when I was married the children got it. [William]

and encouraged us to help others and see good in all people. For all his considerable wealth he never lost his common touch or his Cockney accent. When we were children he used to take us to the amusement park in Southend. He would of course pay for us to go on any rides, and this would attract other children, for whom he would also pay. Sometimes we would have ten or more total strangers joining us, happily following this source of free rides and ice-creams, a tubby, silver-haired, genial latter-day Pied Piper.'

Indeed, William's empathy with children prompted him to come to the aid of a hospital in Estonia when he heard of its lack of facilities for treating the young during an epidemic. In gratitude, the country's government bestowed on him two honours:

Beeleigh four-poster beds extremely comfortable; only drawback an echo from the roof. So one hears snore twice over. [William]

the Order of the Red Cross of Estonia in 1934, and, in 1938, the Order of the White Star of Estonia. However, Buckingham Palace informed William that, as they were foreign orders, he could not wear them on public occasions.

The best day for the younger Foyles was Friday, when William took any of the family who were in town to lunch at the Trocadero in Shaftesbury Avenue. Bill said: 'I remember the staff at the Troc. Mr Woods, the head waiter, always ready to be the butt of Grandad's jokes, always falling for the electric shock handshake, the bread roll slipped into his pocket. I remember the band always played "The Happy Wanderer", Grandad's favourite song, for us. I remember the pride I felt as a little boy to be associated with such a great and kind, lovable and loved man. And I remember years later,

William, giving children the tour of Beeleigh Abbey

Was taking rather a rough fellow around the Abbey [Beeleigh]. He asked me if I was the caretaker and if all the books in the library came from the Stationery Office. I said yes, and when leaving he said: 'Here you are, gov'nor,' and gave me a penny. [William]

Beeleigh Abbey

after Grandad died, we went back to the Troc to try to maintain the ritual. Mr Woods, still there, served us with tears trickling down his face. We never went back as a family.'

William Foyle died peacefully at his home, Beeleigh Abbey, in 1963. He retained his active interest in the business until the end. Christina recalled that on the day before he died he was chuckling as he read about a well-known public librarian's peculations and somewhat 'unorthodox methods' of acquiring and disposing of his books.

Gilbert Samuel Foyle

F.E. Beresford's portrait of Gilbert Foyle, now hanging in John Foyle's home in Horsham

Gilbert was quite different from his brother: he was retiring, serious and studious, not noted for a sense of humour. His portrait, by F. E. Beresford, shows a pleasant, open face with an aquiline nose, and as one member of staff recalled after his death: 'His inherent warmheartedness was allowed to show increasingly as the years went on.'

While William was the front man at Foyles, Gilbert looked after the stock and controlled the finances. And although he was over-shadowed by William in the public eye, he was nevertheless a quietly sociable man and a 'joiner'. He was a Freeman of the City of London and a member of the Royal Society of Arts, while his appointment diaries make frequent reference to walks and rambles. When he retired in 1948 to Eastbourne, he became a local councillor and member of the Rotary Club.

He was generous throughout his life, giving away the money he made and living modestly. In 1951 he lodged securities with the London County Council worth £20,000 (£400,000 in today's values) to form the Gilbert Foyle Educational Trust, which aimed to help needy students through their university careers.

He was a particularly munificent benefactor to his adopted home town, Eastbourne, which he presented with ninety-five acres of downland at Beachy Head, bought from the Duke of Devonshire. He also gave the town more than £36,000 to provide itself with a new sun lounge and café at the Wish Tower on the front as 'a memorial to the people of Eastbourne who were killed or injured in, and their spirit of endurance against, the bombing of the town by the German air force.' When Eastbourne formed its own brass band in 1950, Gilbert presented it with £975 worth of instruments as a gesture of gratitude to the town in which he had holidayed for thirty years. 'Here there were the men, obviously very keen, and struggling along with few instruments of their own; but they couldn't get the money and nobody seemed to be doing anything. So I thought I would lend a hand,' he told the *Eastbourne Courier*.

Gilbert was life president of the Eastbourne Dickens Fellowship. He was passionate about Charles Dickens and collected first editions of his work, which he left to Eastbourne Borough Council. In 1988, the collection was lodged in the library at the University of Sussex.

In 1910 Gilbert married Ethel Cook whom he had met through William's wife Christina. They had two sons, Eric and John. Gilbert was the only member of his family who could drive, and during the First World War, while William looked after the shop, he served in the Royal Army Service Corps in France, driving munitions and supplies lorries during the battle of the Somme.

With the establishment of Foyles Educational in 1921, as a subsidiary of W. & G. Foyle, Gilbert had his own business to run, which he did so successfully that he was able to help out the parent business particularly during hard times in the 1930s. In 1946, Foyles Educational became independent of W. & G. Foyle, although it remained at the same premises until 1964. Then it moved its head office to a new warehouse in Burgess Hill, West Sussex, although its showrooms and retail bookshop remained at Upper Berkeley Street, near Marble Arch.

After retirement, Gilbert continued to take an active interest in Foyles Educational, whose management was taken over by his sons, Eric and John. He died in 1971.

There is nothing like a sacking or two occasionally to remind the troops who's boss. [Christina]

Christina Foyle

Father and daughter relaxing at Beeleigh Abbey, in 1955

As a child, Christina lived for the day when she could join her father in Charing Cross Road, which she did, aged seventeen, as his secretary and right-hand woman. Even as a youngster she accompanied him on book-auction trips, and was allowed to place the bids.

When she was seven, in 1918, Christina contracted tuberculosis and spent six months in a sanatorium. The experience had a deep impact on her, not only because of the shell-shocked soldiers who were being treated there but because her parents visited her only once, perhaps because the disease was so contagious. She was very lonely and missed a good deal of schooling. For the rest of her life she trusted almost no one and although she had many acquaintances and admirers she made few close friends.

Catherine the Great tried to be as charming as possible to everyone and studied every opportunity of winning the affection of those she suspected of being in the slightest degree ill-disposed towards her. [Christina]

'A great fortune is a great slavery' – Seneca, from The Essays of Montaigne. Christina notes, 'Not for me.'

Father and daughter got on well, and Christina proved a blessing to both William and the business. But she was altogether a more complex person than he. She had inherited his persuasive powers, keen nose for publicity, showmanship and skill as a raconteur. Also like him, she had great presence. Yet she was a much cooler customer. A former employee, Rita Delavigne, who joined Foyles' back office after the Second World War, offers a keenly observed and vivid portrait of her employer:

Miss Foyle always looked 'well-kept'. She had short, black, naturally curly hair and greeny-blue eyes that twinkled (like her father's) – the Irish look – and she had a beautiful smile. She could look very severe, like the Queen, but when she smiled her face lit up.

Miss Foyle was always 'on duty'. She usually wore a straight black or navy skirt (just below the knee length) and a freshly ironed, silky-white blouse (not ironed by her – she had a housekeeper who 'did' for her). She had a slim figure but a big bust, very slim legs, and always wore hand-made shoes (or very expensive ones). She often used to wear the same outfits but always wore good shoes and stockings.

One knew if she was around because of the whiff of a beautiful perfume that wafted in the air either before her entrance or her exit. She would stand with her head slightly to one side and backed off a little – with a 'don't come too close' air – like the Queen again. She had that queenly manner. Queen Christina, I used to think.

She used to walk slowly up the aisle between the book-club letter-openers and the row of typists, of which I was one. If she saw any stray rubber-bands lying on the floor she would bend down to pick them up, smile sweetly at you with a look of 'mustn't be wasteful' on her face and put them on your desk. She had these odd quirks.

Captain Lightoller was the only surviving officer of the Titanic. *His daughter, Mavis, was my bridesmaid in 1938. [Christina]*

Despite a reputation for meanness, particularly in matters of staff pay, Christina could be generous and empathetic. Rita remembered being asked to work overtime when there was an extra abundance of letters, and Christina buying bags of fruit from the stall at the corner of Manette Street:

I remember her putting bags of apricots on the centre of the long table for the staff to share…She once gave me a beautiful orchid she'd worn at some function she'd been to which I was thrilled with…she also gave me some nail-varnish (just after the war these were still luxuries). I always remember her sending me to some cocktail party on her behalf to see what 'free items' might be given away. On my return I said to her, 'I went in open-mouthed and open-armed – but nothing I'm afraid.' She laughed. She had a sense of humour that I shared.

Gloria Rouse worked for her at Beeleigh Abbey for twenty years until Christina's death, in the latter ten as her personal secretary. She, too, remembered her employer's sense of humour, and also that Christina was quite different at Beeleigh: 'In the shop she was stern, but at Beeleigh she never told you off, never gave advice. Down here she wore trousers and old shoes – she was comfortable because she was at home, with her animals. I always remember one of the luncheons when I came up behind her. She turned, saw me and said: "Oh, it's you! I was just going to put my voice on."'

Christina rarely failed to make an impact on those who did not know her so well. Sir Arthur Bliss was one among many to pay tribute to his

I went with Princess Alice to visit a hospital. We went into a ward to the bedside of a man and the Princess said, 'Tell me, my man, what is your name?' And he said: 'Hopityoubitch.' The Princess said, 'Oh! So you are a Russian!' [Christina]

I was sitting with friends at the Frankfurt Book Fair many years ago and Sir Stanley Unwin joined us. Someone asked him if he would like a drink and Sir Stanley said, 'No, thanks – I tried it once and didn't enjoy it.' He was then asked if he would like a cigarette and again he said, 'No, thanks – tried smoking once and didn't enjoy it.' After a time, Sir Stanley's son [Rayner Unwin] joined us. Sir Stanley introduced his son to everyone and when it came to the turn of the person offering the drink and cigarettes, he said, 'Your only child, I presume.' [Christina]

hostess at a luncheon in his honour: 'On meeting her, I knew at once that she was not only a very attractive woman, but also – a very rare thing in either men or women – a successful person who does not tell you about it.'

Her nephew Christopher remembered that she and his grandfather never forgot people who had helped them out in difficult times.

Heinemann had not foreclosed on the shop when the going was tough in the 1930s; Tommy Joy of Hatchards had helped sort out a compromise deal in 1965 between Christina and the trade unions. John Dettmer, of Heinemann, and Tommy Joy, with their wives, were subsequently invited to every Foyles Literary Luncheon.

William's propensity for self-promotion was even more pronounced in his daughter. In 1930, aged nineteen, she began to hold the now famous Literary Luncheons. They attracted a huge amount of press coverage over the years because of the quality and profile of the speakers, many of whom were politicians, but Christina gave numerous interviews in her own right as one of the few businesswomen of her generation. She was also an indefatigable traveller. When she was twenty-one, her father sent her to the Soviet Union to collect bad debts. The sights were splendid, but it was not an easy trip. In a letter to her mother she wrote of the magnificence of the Tsar's palace in

CHURCHMAN'S CIGARETTES

MISS CHRISTINA FOYLE

ALBUMS FOR CHURCHMAN'S PICTURE
CARDS CAN BE OBTAINED FROM
TOBACCONISTS AT ONE PENNY EACH

"IN TOWN TO-NIGHT"

A SERIES OF 50

14

MISS CHRISTINA FOYLE
Bookseller

The younger daughter of Mr. W. A. Foyle, Miss Christina Foyle is a partner in the famous firm of W. & G. Foyle, Ltd., the largest second-hand booksellers in the world. All her life she has lived among three million books and in order to keep up their stock, Miss Foyle goes to every country in Europe and the Near East to buy books. She organizes the very successful Foyle's Literary Luncheons, which started with two hundred people and now boast an attendance of fifteen hundred or more. Practically every celebrity has spoken there, and on every possible subject. Miss Foyle's hobbies are Yachting, Reading and skating.

W.A.& A.C.CHURCHMAN

ISSUED BY THE IMPERIAL TOBACCO CO
(OF GREAT BRITAIN & IRELAND) LTD

Christina became so well known as bookseller, organiser of the Literary Luncheons and world traveller that Churchman's included her in its 'In Town To-Night' series of cigarette cards

I don't like asking permission to do something when I don't have to. [Christina]

St Petersburg (then Leningrad), but also of the hardships:

There is no luxury whatever here. There are no proper shops, and people wait in queues yards long for their bread and tobacco…I have nearly been arrested twice. Once for throwing a cigarette end in the gutter and then for crossing October Square, where the public was not allowed.

Her father had given her some addresses at which to call:

The guides did not want me to go, but I said I would be alright [sic]. First I went to the University. The professor I wanted was not there, so I left a catalogue. One of the men was very nice and said he would take me to the other people on my list. The next was in the worst part of Leningrad. There was a whole lot of flats in a smelly, dark courtyard, half of them looked desolate [sic]. I told the man to go because it was getting late and I went in. It was almost dark and I was rather frightened. On the first flight there was a man prostrate, dead drunk with vodka – you see these people lying all over the streets. I knocked and an unpleasant depraved-looking man came. I spoke to him in English but he obviously did not understand and I was so frightened I just turned

Radclyffe Hall, the famous author of The Well of Loneliness, *was a lesbian and lived with Lady Una Troubridge. She said to me: 'You are the only woman I know who enjoys financial independence and complete freedom.' [Christina]*

and fled... Tell Daddy, I'll do my best in Moscow, but it is terribly difficult. I feel so tired and exhausted. They never let us rest.

Some years later, the Russian ambassador asked her to set up in London an exhibition of two thousand Russian books as part of the celebrations for the fiftieth anniversary of the Soviet Union, and two Russians from Moscow were invited to staff the exhibition. They were charming and came as guests to a Literary Luncheon. Christina asked them why they did not defect and stay in England. The Russians replied, 'Miss Foyle, you have in your country a saying "East, West – home's best", and that is

what we believe.' In due course the exhibition closed. 'I was surprised months later to receive a visit from a member of the Special Branch of Scotland Yard who said that the Russians had never returned to Russia,' Christina observed.

In 1942 she was invited to speak to the Royal Dublin Society – 'It was wonderful going to a neutral country whilst we were at war' – and had tea with the President of the Republic, Éamon de Valera. The following year she was asked back. When she arrived there were drinks and she had a 'Clover Club', which 'tasted like lemonade', followed by another. By the time she had to speak she couldn't utter a word: 'I was quite drunk. They never asked me again.'

In the twenties and thirties there was a famous shop called Drage's. The daughter of the owners, Peggy Drage, was a friend of mine and Sir Benjamin and Lady Drage used to give dinner parties and would give me £50 to bring people like famous authors such as J. B. Priestley and Edgar Wallace. They got £50 too! [Christina]

Coming back from America in 1936 my father lost £2000 to card sharps. He told them he had no cash so they asked for a cheque. I asked the Captain to put me ashore early at Plymouth when I telephoned Barclays not to meet the cheque. [Christina]

Christina generally preferred animals to people. She had a succession of dogs, among them a powerful, strong-willed standard poodle named Oscar, who could be seen dragging Christina's faithful friend and housekeeper, Mrs Jacques, in and out of the butcher's shops in Soho. Karl Lawrence, a publisher who lived in Manette Street in the late sixties, recalled the day his miniature dachshund, Jasmine, went missing. After a fruitless search up and down Charing Cross Road and through Soho, he went to Foyles and asked if anyone had seen her. 'As if it was a most natural question to ask in a bookshop, the assistant replied, "Yes, she's upstairs." And there she was, in the flat, sitting on Christina's lap drinking from a saucer of

milk.' By the time of her death, Christina had fifteen cats, several tortoises, a noisy gaggle of peacocks and a snappy dog with a taste for accountants and lawyers.

When her mother's health declined Christina and Ronald maintained the flat in the bookshop building but moved permanently to Beeleigh Abbey. She continued to go up to London to engage staff and for the Literary Luncheons until she died in June 1999.

Christina left a bookshop of almost unbelievable idiosyncrasy: its eccentric retail practices, such as books displayed by publisher rather than author or subject, and a payment procedure that entailed queuing twice, at two separate tills, to make one purchase, charmed and antagonised the customers in equal measure. She had been the power behind William's throne then the undisputed head – dictator – of the business for more than forty years.

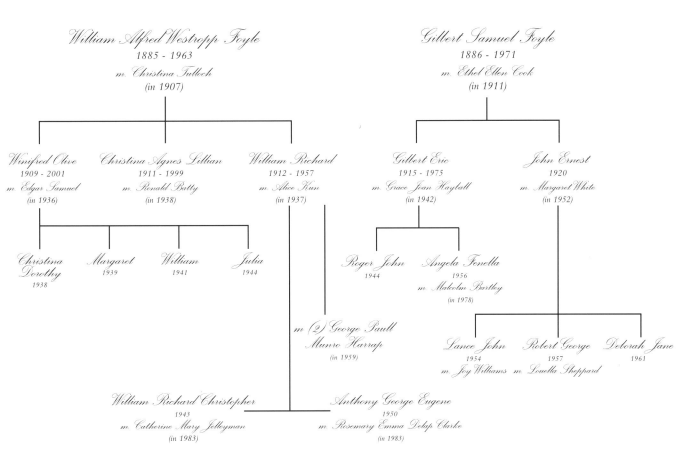

William Alfred Westropp Foyle
1885 - 1963
m. Christina Tulloch
(in 1907)

Gilbert Samuel Foyle
1886 - 1971
m. Ethel Ellen Cook
(in 1911)

Winifred Olive
1909 - 2001
m. Edgar Samuel
(in 1936)

Christina Agnes Lillian
1911 - 1999
m. Ronald Batty
(in 1938)

William Richard
1912 - 1957
m. Alice Kun
(in 1937)

Gilbert Eric
1915 - 1975
m. Grace Jean Hayball
(in 1942)

John Ernest
1920
m. Margaret White
(in 1952)

Christina Dorothy
1938

Margaret
1939

William
1941

Julia
1944

Roger John
1944

Angela Fenella
1956
m. Malcolm Bartley
(in 1978)

m (2) George Paull Munro Harrap
(in 1959)

Lance John
1954
m. Joy Williams

Robert George
1957
m. Louella Sheppard

Deborah Jane
1961

William Richard Christopher
1943
m. Catherine Mary Jelleyman
(in 1983)

Anthony George Eugene
1950
m. Rosemary Emma Delap Clarke
(in 1983)

WORKING AT FOYLES

Telephone conversation overheard:
'I should love to help you,
but I'm Philosophy. Religion
has gone to lunch.'

A staff outing to Epping Forest in 1913. William's elder
daughter, Winifred, and his dog, Wallace, are in the foreground

'A recurring dream of mine, even up to a few years ago, was to find myself back working at Foyles. In what capacity, the dream never made clear, but it always left me with a curious sense of relief.' [Former employee]

Eccentrics drawn to eccentricity

Practically every visitor

to pre-war Foyles, and certainly those to the Theological Department, would have made the acquaintance of its manager. In the shop's early years William bought the Reverend Dr D. G. Duncan's library and took him on too. William made good use of this 'wonderful and most forceful' Baptist preacher, who had a marvellous way of bringing Foyles into his sermons – for which Foyles paid him a guinea a time.

Dr Duncan was clearly an asset. He seemed to know about the doctrines and publications of the most obscure religious bodies, and he had a retentive memory for the most ephemeral pamphlet or sermon in the realm of theology. He was also a man after William's heart: 'Dr Duncan asked me to preside at a Temperance Meeting one Sunday. He suggested a collection, which came to about 17/6d in coppers. Walking home, he said, "You know, Foyle, I feel rather dry." So do I, Doctor, I replied, and we went into a famous hotel. He ordered a bottle of Scotch, which he paid for out of the collection.' Dr Duncan retired in July 1930 at the age of eighty-five after twenty-two years' service to Foyles.

It is in the nature of bookselling to attract colourful characters, and Foyles has certainly employed its fair share. In the early thirties a woman was engaged to head the department that dealt with the occult and alternative philosophies. She came into the shop each day with a parrot perched on her shoulder. Christina turned a blind eye to this until the parrot began to annoy customers. The manager

---

STAFF RULES 1985

It is the policy of Foyles to win the highest possible reputation for genuine courtesy – such courtesy as really well-bred people would show to visitors to their own homes.

Terms of Employment
Employment is on a weekly basis.

Loan of Books
In no circumstances may a member of the staff borrow books. Books from stock may not be taken from the premises during lunchtimes.

Cash
Under no circumstances may assistants pay bills or take money to the cash desk. Assistants must not handle any cash whatsoever, whether customers are buying, selling or returning books. Anyone breaking this very strict rule will be instantly dismissed.

No Exchanges
Books cannot be exchanged after purchase, nor can customers be credited for books returned.

Engaged an assistant to run the department on Health. He said one must dress simply to live long. He appeared daily in open shirt (hairy chest!), shorts and sandals. Customers complained. He eventually died of pneumonia age 32. [Christina]

refused to leave it at home because she was under the impression that her bird had some 'mysterious power'. She was asked to leave.

Her behaviour was no less eccentric than Christina's reason for engaging her in the first place. Under the heading 'Booksellers Who Go Insane', *Reynolds Illustrated News* ran a story on the 'many' salesmen in London bookshops who were losing their jobs because of the 'lure of books'. In the case of books about black magic, Indian philosophy and demonology, they might also 'become mentally unbalanced'. Christina was quoted at length on her salesmen's inability to resist the temptation to study the books they

were selling and how this led to absent-mindedness and neglect of duty; 'So, for a change, we tried a woman.'

The Philately Department, a former employee of the 1950s recalled, was run by a Mr Miller, commonly known as the Stamp Man. 'He fitted the department as though he was made for it – a real Dickensian old man (though he was probably only in his late fifties at the time). He used to arrive at the shop, always on time, wearing a bowler hat and an old raincoat both of which were originally black but were now green with old age.' Other strange characters included a typist who wore long, full skirts and Turkish slippers with turned-up toes; and a woman who typed invoices: 'She used to sit bolt upright, balancing a sort of bird's nest of hair on one side of her head. She had very small bony hands and typed furiously all day long and never spoke.' There was also white-haired, kindly Mrs Turner, who had had a wooden leg since a wartime bombing raid: she presided over Foyles' lift, a creaky, temperamental device with manually operated metal gates that required considerable strength to open them. For many years – she was well into her seventies when she retired – she sat on a stool in the corner and pushed a lever forwards for up and backwards for down.

Gilbert Fabes, author of the whimsical *Autobiography of a Book*, ran the Rare Books Department and contributed elegant, partisan articles to *Foylibra*. In 1930 he wrote, with some enthusiasm, about the bright side of the recent Wall Street collapse:

The joy of the game [book collecting] was in great danger of being spoiled by the wealthy buyers of books. The sport of boxing was turned into a loathsome affair by huge purses…And so with book collecting – cleansed, let us hope, of interlopers with too much money to spend, no love for books and an overwhelming influence upon the markets. We can now, perhaps, settle down to steady business for many years to come with prices for all books at their right level.

I can aver that Messrs Foyles have never attempted to exploit the book lover or collector, and that prices in their establishments have been and always will be at fair market value.

We used to give brandy to those who fainted, but so frequent we changed over to sal-volatile. Fainters became less. [William]

There was Albert Dowsett, of the maintenance staff, who, even on the coldest day with all his overcoats under his overall, kept a sunny temperament. Frederick Bell recalled developing 'a sort of cross-talk act' with Albert, which they used, 'sometimes unkindly', to get the local ladies of the night to move on rather than hang about getting in the way of customers – until a woman reported Fred to the manager, who ticked him off in front of her. She departed 'greatly mollified'.

Later on there were two very different general managers: the much-respected Mr Rush, and the much-feared Velimir Stimac, who would keep senior publishers' representatives queuing outside his fourth-floor office like so many naughty schoolboys.

Never let staff put up paper chains in the shop at Christmas. [Christina]

Looking Back

The invaluable Dr Duncan, manager of the Theology Department, with Gilbert Foyle

Foyles seems to leave

an indelible mark on everyone who has worked there. Former employees' reminiscences suggest that they felt as though they belonged to a unique club. Rita Delavigne joined, aged twenty, as William's secretary just after the Second World War:

I thought I had died and gone to heaven, after working during the war in the planning office of an aircraft factory making Hurricane bombers, where everything was 'hush-hush'. Every bit of correspondence had to be double-checked before being posted, and everything was rationed, so when I first asked for a shorthand book and pencil from the stationery cupboard at Foyles I was looking round for a book to sign when someone said, 'What are you looking for?' and I told them. There was a blank look of amusement and the reply, 'Help yourself, take what you want.' I felt really guilty. Habits die hard.

The first day I was there, Mr William Foyle – WF we used to call him – dictated replies to piles of letters he'd received from all over the world, all simple letters but lots of them, and, as I had always done at my previous job, I made a neat pile of them with envelopes attached, together with carbon copies for the file and took them into his office for him to sign. I can remember Miss Foyle looking across at me quizzically but not interfering, and Mr Foyle looking up at me with an amused expression. Waving me off, he said, 'You sign 'em.' 'Don't you want to look at them?' 'You know your trouble, you're too conscientious!' When I asked where the filing cabinet was he just took the carbon copies and tore them all up.

The staff were allowed to purchase books every Friday from WF, so there was always a queue outside his office. He used to allow a third off the price, but as an added attraction – Mr Foyle often used to bring produce up from Beeleigh Abbey – he had a whole pile of boxes of lettuces on his desk, and as you left he would say in his high-pitched voice, 'Take a lettuce, then.' This never failed to amuse me: it was so 'cosy'.

Engaged a chauffeur name Barnes. Went away on holiday and arranged for him to start on return. When he called, the maid announced, 'Barnes.' I forgot the engagement and thought he was one of my friends. I asked him in to dinner and wine etc. He didn't say much. After entertaining him, he said, 'When do I start?' I said, 'Start what?' He said, 'Driving,' and then I tumbled to it. [William]

In those days, whenever there was an exhibition in the Art Department Miss Foyle used to ask some of the staff to put on their coats and pretend to be visitors if only a few people turned up. A very kind and thoughtful gesture, I used to think, to save the face of the artist.

Once, word went round that Marlene Dietrich was in the Rare Books Department, so I beckoned to my friend Daphne, who was the telephonist at Foyles, and made a quick run down the stairs to get a glance at her. She wore a little pill-box hat tilted over one eye but wore a veil pulled tightly over her face and into a bow behind her head. She was so smartly dressed in a man-type suit and high heels and of course we were both fascinated to hear her lovely low German-accented voice. To see her in person in such a personal setting was a real treat. So many famous people visited Foyles – The Famous Bookshop.

If you couldn't find a book elsewhere you could bet you would discover one on Foyles' shelves. Of course, you had to hunt for it, and then look around for the cloakroom to wash your very dusty hands.

Books were still out of print and Foyles dealt mainly in second-hand copies – so many of which were treasures. And this was the atmosphere I walked into, a dusty old-fashioned bookshop with miles and miles of dusty shelves covered in 'treasures to seek for'. I will never forget the smell, which if I close my eyes, fifty years later, I can always recall immediately.

Another ex-employee, Derek Scott, wrote several entertaining columns, drawing on his Foyles days, for *Credit Management*, the journal of the Institute of Credit Management. He described his first days at the bookshop, running the sales ledger of the mail-order business. He was put in the charge of a young man who, it

I always sack a person when he becomes indispensable. [Christina]

A dear lady was discharged as not being quite suitable. She seemed quite satisfied, but on the Friday evening she came into my office and exclaimed: 'Goodbye, Mr Foyle, may your soul burn in hell.' [William]

turned out, was 'family'. His mentor was both charming and helpful: 'He reminded me in some way of the upper-class hero from children's adventure stories. He was later to be involved with planes, and maybe my pet name of "Biggles" was very apt. My abiding memory is "flying" with him through Hyde Park Underpass in his sports car, well in excess of the speed limit. He remarked casually that he was in a hurry as he was expected in Court in the afternoon on a speeding charge!' 'Biggles' was Christopher Foyle.

Another of Derek's abiding memories concerned Hans, a warehouseman. Hans was leaving the company, and, after a farewell drink, was discovered in the building wearing no trousers. After a fruitless search for them Derek returned to his office and credit-related matters. Suddenly he looked up to find Hans, reunited

with his trousers, standing before him. 'He leant over and, while tweaking my nose with one hand, he scattered the remnants of his clocking-in card over me like confetti with the other, muttering, "Capitalist pig."'

With its large staff, all mainly under one roof, Foyles was the ideal environment for making new friends and socialising. According to Richard Lewis, who ran Foyles Transport Department in 1998-9, 'We spent a lot of time and energy flirting with each other – in person, by phone or on paper. Everybody did. There was one ageing Lothario who reckoned he spoke every European language. When a new pretty girl started he could be seen conversing enthusiastically with them in their language. We were all impressed and very jealous, until one of his victims told us he was explaining to her all about military history.

'One boy asked a girl out over the internal phone. She agreed, but then later dumped him over the internal phone too – she had thought he was someone else. One girl gave me lessons in Greek. I exchanged notes with another in Icelandic and we both decoded them with our Icelandic dictionaries from the second floor.'

Foyles was – and still is – very proud of the international nature of its staff. Occasionally it listed the languages spoken by its employees in *Foylibra* – in 1970, for example, Arabic, Czech, Danish, Finnish, French, German, Greek, Hebrew, Hindustani, Italian, Maltese, Norwegian, Polish, Portuguese, Russian, Serbo-Croat, Slovak, Spanish and Swedish. As a matter of policy Christina hired students from all over the world as summer and temporary workers in the shop.

Geert-Jan Laan joined Foyles in 1962 as a nineteen-year-old student from the Netherlands. Now editor-in-chief of *Dagblad van het Noorden*,

a major regional newspaper, he has occasionally drawn on the experience for his journalism. At Foyles his was a meteoric rise and an even swifter fall. From a modest start at the Book Club, via the Paperback Department, he reached the zenith of his career when Miss Rosenstiehl – 'she was nearest to the sunshine of Miss Foyle herself' – appointed him manager, United States and Canada.

I had to collect all the books which were ordered by customers in the USA and Canada and ship them over there. But I was also put on commission. Instead of the weekly seven or eight pounds, I could make about fifteen to twenty pounds, which made me a very rich young man at that time in London. Blinded by greed, I soon selected first the orders for the more expensive books. This meant that my turnover shot up. I was even invited into the director's office, where Miss Rosenstiehl proudly showed me that I had sold substantially more than my German predecessor. However, customers who ordered cheap Penguins

*When people come to work for me I lay down the conditions of employment. They may accept them or reject them quite freely as they wish. But **I lay down the conditions.** [Christina]*

*started to complain that their orders did not come
through. And then I made a fatal mistake. I replied to
a furious Texan that he had not yet received his order
probably because of a postal strike in the US. The man
filed a complaint with the British-American Chamber
of Commerce.*

Geert-Jan got his marching orders from the
then general manager Mr Rush. 'Of course, it
was my own fault,' he conceded.

Geert-Jan was not the only student to notice
that 'very few employees of foreign birth lasted
longer than about half a year'. Most members of
staff under Christina's regime received at some
stage the dreaded 'white paper' in the weekly pay
envelope, or were dismissed for some
misdemeanour – Foyles, under Christina, did not
value old retainership.

Indeed, in 1956 there were stirrings of
discontent. Thirty-eight students signed on in
summer jobs for a minimum of six weeks, only
to be given a week's notice on the last day of the
third; thus, they believed, the bookshop avoided
paying a rise due at the beginning of the fifth.
Most were foreign, sent by their parents to learn
English, but one was a spirited music graduate,

Deirdre Ive. She was so incensed by this
treatment, and the impression of Britain that it
had given her fellows, that she and another
British student got up a petition. All thirty-eight
students signed it, but she could not persuade
the permanent staff to add their names, no
matter how sympathetic they were to the cause
– and many were. 'We actually presented the
petition to Miss Foyle in person. I think she just
looked at it and said, "Thank you." Everyone
except the two of us was sacked. I'll never know
why, because it left two politically-minded
animals to cause trouble for the rest of the six
weeks.'

Not everyone held Foyles' employment
conditions against the firm, or even Christina. A
former employee of the late 1950s was moved to
write a supportive letter to Christina in the early
eighties after an attack on her in the press. He
recalled many happy days working at 'the dear
old store': Miss Rosenstiehl discreetly recovering
expensive art books that William had given away
to pretty girls, the scent of lily-of-the-valley that
followed Christina through the shop, and
Christina's generous response to a charity request

('the *only* response from the major book houses in central London'). It was only towards the end of his letter that he disclosed that he had been sacked for poor time-keeping – 'totally deserved in retrospect,' he observed.

One of the few members of staff who survived to qualify as an 'old retainer' was the bookshop's loyal and long-suffering publicity manager, Ben Perrick, who joined Foyles from Harrods in 1934. He worked closely and tirelessly with Christina on well over five hundred Literary Luncheons – Frankie Howerd, the comedian, once referred to him as 'Miss Foyle's minder'.

Ben was also responsible for publicising the Book Clubs, publishing *Foylibra*, and attracting customers to the shop, from home and overseas, and keeping in touch with them. This slight, wiry-haired typhoon of a man, married to the former *Express* and *Mail* columnist Eve Perrick and father of journalist Penny Perrick, was well known and liked in the book trade and in Fleet Street. He retired in 1997, well into his eighties, after nearly sixty-five years with the company.

Many temporary Foyles staff went on to become publishers and booksellers, some holding top jobs. Former bookseller Ian Norrie had the rare pleasure of being employed twice by Christina, once at Foyles and then as manager of the High Hill Bookshop in Hampstead, North London, which she later sold to him. He once received a note from her that read, 'If you were 20 years younger I would give you Foyles.' When he mentioned this to a friend at the Booksellers Association, the reply came: 'I've got one of those letters too.'

Ian concluded his obituary of Christina for *The Bookseller* magazine: 'Working for Christina could be disagreeable; knowing her socially was fun.'

Ben Perrick, Foyles' long-serving publicity manager, hovers discreetly behind Christina and her guest, former Speaker of the House of Commons Lord Tonypandy, at a luncheon on 17 April 1984

Striking Times

William and Gilbert were good employers and took pleasure in seeing their staff enjoying themselves. One of the annual highlights was the concert and dance given by the directors. The twentieth, in 1929, was the biggest and best yet, attended by 350 members of staff. The Clarion Syncopators, under the able direction of Mr A. R. Smith, played the newest tunes and old favourites; Mr Harold Finch led the community singing; Dr Duncan proposed a hearty vote of thanks to the directors, 'to which we assented with three rousing cheers. Then, led by Mr Bradley, we shook the roof with "For They Are Jolly Good Fellows".'

The following year saw the inauguration of the Foylibra Social Club, which aimed to offer ping-pong, darts, tiddlywinks, bridge, whist and dominoes; for the more energetic members, there were country rambles, and dancing to a gramophone lent by the music company. There were regular outings further afield, too – Thames cruises, a trip to Margate. William's elder daughter Winifred was in charge of the club and through it met her husband Edgar Samuel.

A quarter of a century later, Christina tried to revive the idea and bought a large Georgian farmhouse in Essex for the use of staff at weekends. The experiment was short-lived: they did not treat the house with the respect Christina thought it deserved, and it was sold. Christina's attitude to her employees was more ambivalent than that of her father and uncle. While many of the permanent staff – the back-room workers and departmental managers – were devoted to the company, the times were changing.

Christina did not appreciate the new sixties breed of job seeker: 'Every hippie and similar person, having got tired of hanging about and doing nothing for six months of a year, thinks, Well, it would be rather fun to work in a bookshop. So in they come, bells jangling, and lounging in my uncomfortable office chair, their extraordinary cigarette smoke filling the office. They say, "But I'm mad about books, I'm just the person for this job." We get this once a week.

Occasionally, when we are either distraught for staff or simply berserk, we have taken one on. The things that happen when you do are really frightening. I have heard one of my best and most serious customers, a woman, being spoken to as "Say, ma'am, now you listen to me..."'

Foyles' somewhat cavalier post-war employment practices did not go unchallenged in the political climate of the 1960s and in May 1965 Christina had a strike on her hands. More than a hundred employees walked out over pay and conditions, with the backing of the Union of Shop, Distributive and Allied Workers (USDAW). The strike was triggered by the sacking of twenty-two-year-old Australian Marius Webb for unpunctuality.

This time Christina's gift for providing the press with quotes and other material that would boost Foyles deserted her. The *Evening Standard* reported her as having said: 'Nothing like this has ever happened before. I run the firm as a trust for my father, and I could chuck it up and be a millionaire tomorrow if I wanted to be.' In answering complaints that Foyles did not pay sick leave, and sometimes sacked sick members of the staff, she said: 'We get a lot of layabouts. If they are away very much we sack them, but we don't sack people who are any good.' When the strike had lasted three weeks, Foyles agreed to recognise the union, as a voluntary option for staff, and grant a pay increase.

Seventeen years later, in 1982, Foyles was again under attack as staff tried to regain union recognition: union membership had dwindled in the intervening years as the right to permanent employment was never secured. When two employees were fired for joining USDAW, the pickets were out once more. This time Christina, now aged seventy-one, kept a low profile, although again she threatened to close down the bookshop. It was clear that she had never understood how anyone could complain about working at Foyles. Eventually, the pickets were lifted but not before a letter had appeared in the *Guardian*, signed by seventy writers, actors and academics – including frequent speaker and guest J. B. Priestley – protesting at Foyles' employment policy and threatening to boycott the Literary Luncheons.

Foyles' response to the strike was to ask prospective employees to sign a 'take us as you find us agreement' recognising that there were no canteen facilities, no training and that the conditions might be a bit dusty.

During the strikes vilification and support came to Christina in equal measure. In 1965 she received the following from an anonymous well-wisher: 'Don't give up, Miss Foyle. The people concerned have been paid to cause trouble. Somebody wants your shop very badly; don't give in. It is a disgraceful business. They are lucky to receive £10 per week. Why not recruit older men and women, Britons who need work and who would give good value for money? Good luck.' The incumbent of a Scottish diocese suggested: 'Why not sack the lot?'

Nowadays Foyles offers a very different working environment. The shop, inside and out, and its employment practices have been transformed. The profile of the floor staff is different too. Most significantly, they are all engaged on a permanent basis: Foyles no longer recruits temporary or seasonal workers. Instead, the company looks for previous bookselling experience (or good customer-service experience in a similar retail environment) and for people who want to make a career in bookselling or publishing. More than 90 per cent have first degrees and many have masters'.

Foyles still prides itself on the number of foreign languages spoken by its staff, which today include Afrikaans, Cantonese, Danish, Dutch, Farsi, French, German, Greek, Hebrew, Hindi, Italian, Portuguese, Serbian, Spanish, Swedish and Urdu. The bookshop recruits in the main via its website and from unsolicited CVs – it only advertises in the press for specialist positions. Thanks to the Foyles name, there is a steady stream of applicants, often from rival bookshops.

Foyles invests in its staff, offering a package that compares well with the other major booksellers: a competitive salary, contract, decent holiday entitlement and training. And, of course, all staff are allowed to carry out cash and card transactions with customers.

The right person wanted for bookselling: good secondary school, not university. Languages useful. Secret of being a good bookseller is handling stock. You get to know it without realising it. We have three million books in our place, and I think my father could pick out any one at any time. [Christina]

CHAPTER 3

FOYLES
AT WAR

V Bombs were dropping all around Tottenham Court Road. Was in a bus and the bus in front went up in the air. Wrigleys [chewing gum] premises blown up and about 27 people killed. [William]

Members of HM Forces browsing in the shop

Can often foretell coming events in the political world by the type of book being asked for, especially from abroad. For instance, Foyles knew that Russia was coming into the last war: we were being asked for books on the Russian–Japanese war, aircraft, guns. Japan the same: long before she came in Japan bought up all our books on armaments, submarines etc. Germany, just before war broke out, wanted every map and plan of defences of London against air attack. [William]

A close shave

From the outbreak of the

Second World War, Foyles and its staff threw themselves into the war effort. A steady stream of personnel, both men and women, left to join up. In late 1940 the departure of the shop's general manager for the Navy was celebrated by *Foylibra* with the headline: 'Warning to U-Boats – Tom Langdon's in the Navy!' The family were no exception. William's son Dick joined the Royal Naval Volunteer Reserve and ultimately became a lieutenant in command of motor vessels in the Mediterranean, North Africa and the North Atlantic. Gilbert, in the Home Guard, saw both his sons enlist: Eric in the Signals Section of the RAF; and John in the Royal Engineers.

Meanwhile, members of the armed forces on leave could be found browsing the shelves. On a single day in the summer of 1940 Foyles' Technical Department recorded among its visitors several Anzacs, a Norwegian seaman, a Polish flying officer, and Canadian, Dutch, French and Cypriot soldiers.

Parcels of books were dispatched to where they were most needed – to wounded French soldiers and sailors in British hospitals, to the RAF, British Red Cross and many other organisations around the world. A thank-you letter was received from British prisoners-of-war in Germany: 'We are sure that the sight of men taking their ease at the weekend, after the week's toil, would be gratifying to you, could you but see them in the rather crowded quarters of a hay-loft above a stable, reading your books.'

Encouraged by the British Ship Adoption Society, Foyles' staff adopted a steamship on coastal work, the SS *Tielbank*, and sent games, books and 'comforts' to the seamen; customers were encouraged to come up with reading material, 'preferably novels', for them. The staff followed the progress of the ship towards its unrevealed destinations in *Foylibra*. In August 1940 *Tielbank* returned safely to London after an absence of six months 'with many thrilling stories to tell'. During their stay Gilbert entertained the crew. Sadly the *Tielbank* was sunk in 1941, whereupon he announced the adoption of the *Myrtlebank*.

The war touched Foyles more closely still when the Blitz was unleashed. In autumn 1940 a high-explosive bomb fell immediately outside the Charing Cross Road premises leaving a large crater close to the shop. William arrived at work to find a block of concrete on his desk and his typewriter on top of a cupboard. The sappers were soon on the scene, building a Bailey bridge

Visitors to the shop 1940/41 included: Ursula Bloom, Jessie Matthews, Compton Mackenzie, Sybil Thorndike, Graham Greene, Hilaire Belloc, Dennis Wheatley, Elinor Glyn, Clive Brook, George Formby, Vera Brittain, Noël Coward, Edith Evans, the Emperor of Ethiopia

Books make good filling for sandbags in 1940. Meanwhile, up on the roof *Mein Kampf* was protecting the building against German bombs

General Sir Alan Brooke, Commander-in-Chief of the Home Forces: 'I have had brought to my notice your very generous treatment of the 684th General Construction Coy. of the Royal Engineers...I desire to thank you for your kindness to them, and for the way in which you have encouraged them in their duty.'

Later William recalled the opening ceremony – at which one of his many brushes with the authorities had occurred: 'We called it Foyle Bridge. Just as I was about to cut the ribbon in front of all the press photographers and reporters, the local surveyor approached me and said: "What the dickens are you doing? This is my bridge or the Holborn Bridge." I said "No, it's *my* bridge!" He said, "You can't do this etc." Daughter Christina luckily came along. I winked and she tactfully led him away till the deed was done.'

The book business in general was less fortunate than Foyles had been. More than ten million books were destroyed in London alone during the Blitz, and the then heart of publishing, Paternoster Row, was devastated. The premises of *Foylibra*'s printers, S. Tinsley &

across the crater. By the time it was completed William had persuaded the major in charge to call it the Foyle Bridge. Naturally there was a ribbon-cutting ceremony accompanied by a photo-call for the newspapers.

Clearly William had been a generous host to the bridge-building soldiers for shortly afterwards the following letter arrived from

Co., took a hit, but its staff managed somehow to continue printing.

William appears to have relished these dangerous and uncertain times. He recorded:

During air raids, wife, daughter Christina and all staff were wonderful. They all carried on as usual tho' morning after morning when we arrived, found all the windows out and the place full of debris. Wife and family refused to leave London and the staff refused to go to the basement. During one raid, the maid at home set herself alight. The wife pluckily put out the flames and phoned police and ambulance. I thought I was in Hades or Dante's Inferno. Maid screaming and bombs dropping all round. Shared a bottle of Scotch with the police force.

Yet despite the bombs and other wartime difficulties, Foyles continued to expand, with a big new Book Club operation. Early in the war it celebrated reaching 200,000 members with a luncheon at which speakers included J. B. Priestley and Harold Macmillan, MP. Throughout the war books were despatched from the clubs to prisoners-of-war; Book Club issues were read in Tobruk during the siege, and in 1944 soldiers applied for membership from the Anzio beachhead in Italy.

Ever the showman, William never missed an opportunity. In the early days of the Third Reich, when Adolf Hitler announced that he was going to have all Jewish books burnt, Foyles sent him a telegram offering to buy them. The cable read: 'Do not burn those books. Sell them to us and we will give you good price, which you can devote to German youth movement.'

Back came the reply: 'Would no sooner corrupt the morals of the English than the Germans.'

In his quiet way Gilbert also liked to make his mark. He wrote a 'stirring' new marching song with music by Gerald Vall, 'With A Laugh And A Song', which was played on *Music While You Work* and by orchestras nationwide.

Christina kept herself busy with talks to women's and other groups up and down the country. Her appeal to Book Club members to send their unwanted books for pulping met with an immediate response, and many tons were sent to the mills to be turned into 'valuable material to aid the war effort'. Among them were several

Enquiries received for books on Love Potions, Manufacture of Adhesive Tape, Earthquakes, the Wars of the Roses, Onions [William]

copies of Hitler's *Mein Kampf*, which, satisfyingly, helped to meet 'the great need for paper to feed the war machines'. (The paper-quota restrictions for books were not lifted until March 1949.)

The staff, too, did their bit for the war effort. Irene Hatter of the Accounts Department answered the Ministry of Agriculture's call to 'Dig for Victory': she converted a neglected back garden into a flourishing vegetable patch, producing a good crop of potatoes, cabbages, beans, lettuces and beetroot. 'Admirable wartime effort, Miss Hatter!' boomed the editor of *Foylibra*.

Foylibra triumphed early on with a back cover that attracted the attention of the Ministry of Information as 'first-rate reading, and just the kind of thing we want people abroad to know':

Let us tell you what it is like in London. We – if anyone – should know, for we are Cockneys born and bred, working daily in the very heart of London, sleeping nightly in the outlying suburbs. And we can assure you beyond all doubt that London and Londoners have their chins well up. People are working with more purpose, more determination. Otherwise, life in the Capital continues very much as usual. The main shopping streets still attract their bustling crowds. Restaurants, cinemas and stores are busy. Shoeblacks still shine shoes in Piccadilly Circus. And in Hyde Park, elderly gentlemen still snooze in chairs. But what of Foyles itself? Well, in this bookshop we are very, very busy. Several departments are 'up' on their pre-war figures. In fact 'blitzkrieg' or no 'blitzkrieg', Foyles remains a very good bookshop indeed.

Encouraged by the Ministry other back covers followed in similar morale-boosting tone. Occasionally the editor of *Foylibra* got carried away:

> ## WE MAY BE WRONG!
> Of course, we may be wrong. Perhaps there is someone, somewhere in the world who has not heard of Foyles. Perhaps it is mere coincidence that our post includes letters from Acton and Abatamagomaw, from Kafiristan and Kensal Green, from Manchester and Mynddislwyn. But we like to think that they do know us in these places. That the business man in his office, the native in his kraal, the soldier in his dug-out, the mandarin in his palace – all have books from our shelves. And when our customers tell us that Foyles is the very best bookshop of all, blushingly we answer – well, we think so too!

'Moral – Always Carry a Dictionary'

How a sixpenny dictionary was instrumental in bringing the 7,000-ton captured Nazi freighter *Uhenfels* to London has been revealed by Captain H. Flowerdew of the British Merchant Navy. 'The Germans made an attempt to scuttle the *Uhenfels* after they had been sighted by a plane from the *Ark Royal*,' Captain Flowerdew said, 'but the Navy boarded her, and to get over the difficulty of navigating a German ship in which all instructions and machinery are German, we used a sixpenny German-English dictionary.' The *Uhenfels* is worth roughly £750,000.

FOYLIBRA, APRIL 1940

'The Publicity He Gets!'

Books dealing with the German Führer are still a feature of almost every London publisher's list. They include *Hitler's Last Year of Power*; *The German People Versus Hitler*; *How to Conquer Hitler*; *Hitler Over Latin America*; *The Hitler Cult and How it Will End*; *I Was Hitler's Prisoner*; *Standing Up to Hitler*; *Hitler Calls This Living*; *Hitler's Route to Baghdad*; *From Nietzsche to Hitler*.

FOYLIBRA, MARCH 1940

Carry on Lunching

The Literary Luncheons

continued throughout the war, offering much-needed opportunities for laughter and a platform for morale-boosting and wartime appeals. Foyles' records of this period reveal the concerns of the moment. Speakers no longer had to be linked with books and were often drawn from other spheres. One of the most prominent guest speakers, in January 1941, was General Charles de Gaulle. He made a memorably rousing call to his fellow countrymen to rally round the Cross of Lorraine, the emblem of the Free French: 'While the British Empire carries in her turn heroically almost the whole weight of this gigantic struggle, Free France contrives so that Frenchmen can struggle at her side either to death or victory.'

Later Christina shed light on the greater significance of the event, which was chaired by Cardinal Hinsley, then Archbishop of Westminster: 'When I asked General de Gaulle to come, he said, "Yes, if you can persuade

Saw the first Zeppelin fly low over London. A man fired at it and was fined for having a gun with no licence! Saw the one come down at Potters Bar. [William]

Cardinal Hinsley to preside." The position with the Catholic Church had been very delicate owing to Pétain [head of the puppet Vichy government of occupied France]. The Cardinal came, and thus brought recognition to the Free French Movement from all Roman Catholics both in this country and in Canada.'

Later that year J. B. Priestley was campaigning for freedom of expression and looking to longer-term social changes: 'Let us look forward rather than backward, because whatever happens we are never going to make the people of Europe stand up and defy the Gestapo by asking them to do so on behalf of the Eton and Harrow match at Lords, Ascot, the Boat Race and other specifically English functions – and yet that is the kind of mind we get.'

Food was obviously a matter of intense interest, and advice was forthcoming at a

Literary Luncheon at the Grosvenor House Hotel in July 1940. The head chef, Gabriel Vallet, took up the challenge of cooking a meal that cost ninepence a head for the guests, while the speaker, Vicomte de Mauduit, author of *They Can't Ration These*, provided some useful culinary tips: 'How many of us know that the young shoots of the common bracken or the tips of wild hop can be as delicious as asparagus? Or that the clover, the nettle, the dandelion, the yarrow can make nourishing soups, tasty purées and refreshing salads? Or that the hedgehog and the grey squirrel can make pleasurable roasts, stews and pies?'

The luncheons were splendid opportunities for humour of a very British kind. Gerald Kersh, author of *They Die With Their Boots Clean*, regaled guests with a story that was then doing the rounds. A ferocious but bored captain with a certain famous infantry regiment in North Africa had set off into the desert to fight the Germans with only a camel and a two-way radio. After some time, headquarters in Alexandria received a communiqué in code: 'I have captured Rommel; send advice – Smith'.

When all Paternoster was destroyed, went to call on a well-known publisher. He was sitting on a Tate sugar box amidst the ruins, checking up accounts: still cheerful and smiling. [William]

They returned a message in code saying: 'Congratulations, magnificent job of work. Hold him! Arrangements being made for reception in Alexandria. May rely upon DSO at least. Signed, General.' The bunting was hung out in Alexandria and they waited for the appearance of Smith and Rommel. Nothing happened. Eventually a faint message came through: 'Do not understand; please repeat.' The message was repeated and they waited for several more days. Then very, very faintly the reply arrived: 'Do not quite understand what you mean. I will repeat my message. I have ruptured camel: what shall I do?'

There were many tales of derring-do. In September 1943, Theador Broch, the mayor of Narvik, gave a first-hand account of the capture, rescue and reoccupation of his town as the Allies tried to keep a foothold in Norway. With the Allied ring tightening around Narvik, the German occupying forces became harsher. One night, when shots were fired against German soldiers, Broch was ordered to pick out five important persons in the town who would be held by the Nazis as a guarantee against any disturbance. 'Of course,' Broch told his audience, 'it was not very nice to pick out five friends to be hostages for the Nazis, but if I hadn't they would have taken ten or twenty and there would have been panic.' He chose himself, the chief of police, the chief doctor, the city engineer and the manager of the Swedish Iron Ore Company,

'Very first person'

Books displayed recently in Foyles main showroom included the following titles: *I Want an Audience*; *I Fell for a Sailor*; *I Spy, Can This Be I?*; *I, Claudius*; *If I Were King*; *I Hate Tomorrow*; *I Liked the Life I Lived*.

FOYLIBRA, DECEMBER 1941

'Blackout Book Boom'

An increase in book sales resulting from the blackout is reported by the *Sunday Dispatch*. At Foyles...from January to March 1939, approximately 500,000 books were sold. This year, over the same period, the figure is well over 750,000.

FOYLIBRA, APRIL 1940

The Foyles van crossing Foyle Bridge, built by Royal Engineers in 1940 over the bomb crater in Charing Cross Road

who was a Norwegian. 'All over the town they had put up posters saying we five had to be shot if anything happened. But all five stayed alive.' Narvik was liberated, then recaptured, and Broch eventually made his escape through a back window and on to Britain.

A home-grown hero, who confessed to an enthusiasm for thrillers, was immediately taken up by Foyles. Captain Robert Davies had led the squad who saved St Paul's Cathedral by removing a time-bomb from its vicinity. His

'Führer Playing Second Fiddle?'

A study of recent political books indicates the likelihood that Chancellor Hitler is being supplanted by Joseph Stalin as the favourite subject of political biographers. Selling well at Foyles are W. G. Krivitsky's *I Was Stalin's Agent*, Boris Souveraine's *Stalin*, A. V. Baikaloff's *I Knew Stalin*, Eileen Bigland's *The Riddle of the Kremlin*.

FOYLIBRA, MAY 1940

'Wedding Bells
for Thomas Langdon, Eileen McGrady'

From their many friends at Foyles, go good wishes to Ordinary Seaman Thomas Langdon and Miss Eileen McGrady, whose marriage is announced for Saturday, June 7th. Before joining the Navy, Mr Langdon was Foyles' general manager. Miss McGrady was Book Club office manageress.

FOYLIBRA, MAY 1941

reward was to be invited to a Literary Luncheon where he was seated next to the famously exotic novelist and short-story writer Mrs Elinor Glyn – the official photograph shows him smiling rather nervously.

One of the more unusual luncheons was held in 1940 when 1500 people turned out to see the celebrities: spies. These included real ones such as Sir Paul Dukes, Captain von Rintelen and Colonel Victor Kaledin, and a clutch of spy writers. Whole pages of photographs of Foyles' 'Secret Service' luncheon subsequently appeared in issues of the *Bystander*, *Tatler* and the *Sketch*.

Although the war continued in the Far East, *Foylibra* thought it fitting to pay tribute where it was due at the time of the VE celebrations in May 1945: 'The staff, in common with so many in London, have shown throughout a steady calm and courage which has proved sufficient for their ordeal, and a spirit worthy of the sacrifice and endurance on the part of Forces everywhere which has made this victory possible.'

In June 1945, a small white goat was spotted strolling sedately down Charing Cross Road. London and Foyles were returning to some kind of normality.

Sun Electric staff look on across the street as the bridge is opened over the bomb crater outside
Foyles. Otherwise, it's business as usual – 'Hitler Can't Put Out the Sun'

'Women must resolve now that they
will not allow themselves to be
ruthlessly flung aside as they were
after the Armistice of 1918…War
gives women the opportunity to show
what they can do, but with the
return of peace their work is
discarded and barriers erected to
confine their activities. The younger
generation must plan now how best
to safeguard women's future. No
profession or work should be barred
to them as women, provided they are
suitable and able.'
[The Marchioness of Londonderry, Foyles
Literary Luncheon, July 1941]

CHAPTER 4

THE
FAMOUS
AND NOT
SO FAMOUS

A lady customer wrote and asked for
every novel in which the heroine
wears spectacles. [William]

In the basement: a member of the public sells her
books to Foyles

'I say that there has never been any other bookshop, and never will be, that has known quite so well as Foyles how to sell books. I have no hesitation in saying that Foyles have done more for authors and readers than any other institution anywhere in the world.' [Sir Compton Mackenzie, June 1957]

Foyles and the Famous

Foyles has been a magnet

for writers, artists, actors, royalty, politicians and all concerned with the arts. Over the years Bernard Shaw, John Masefield, Somerset Maugham, Sir Compton Mackenzie, J. B. Priestley, H. G. Wells, Henry Miller, John Galsworthy, Laurie Lee and Professor J. K. Galbraith were all regular customers. William had several long chats with Queen Mary: 'She has a vast knowledge of rare books and bindings,' he remarked.

At Christmas 1949 and New Year 1950, greetings arrived at the bookshop from the luminaries of diverse fields: A. J. Cronin, Dr Marie Stopes, Enid Blyton, Wilfred Pickles,

Visitors in 1930
Dr Marie Stopes
Prince Eilo of
Montenegro
The Sanbwa of
Mongmit

Visitors 1940
HRH The Princess
Royal
Dennis Wheatley
Ursula Bloom
Hector Bolitho
Jessie Matthews
J. B. Priestley
Sybil Thorndike
Graham Greene
Alastair Sim
Max Miller
Hilaire Belloc

Visitors 1950

Mr Thakin Nu,
Prime Minister of
Burma
Queen Elisabeth of
the Belgians
Noël Coward
Dorothy Sayers
Wilfred Pickles
Brendan Bracken
Marius Goring
Eileen Joyce
John Gielgud
Terence Rattigan
Tyrone Power
Anthony Eden
Enid Blyton

Ursula Bloom, Margaret Lockwood and Dame Sybil Thorndike. A quick dip into 1960s post-bag revealed orders from, among others, Field Marshal Viscount Montgomery, Sir Winston Churchill, Norman Wisdom, Michael Redgrave, Douglas Fairbanks and the Bishop of Exeter. For several years Éamon de Valera paid an annual visit for the latest books on mathematics. Noël Coward claimed that the inspiration for *Cavalcade* had come from some old volumes he had found on Foyles' shelves. Walt Disney often browsed among the fine collection of art books. Lord Morrison of Lambeth, the former cabinet minister Herbert Morrison, said that he gained much of his political education from the books he bought at Foyles, and David Ben-Gurion once spent a whole morning in the Philosophy Department.

President Perón of Argentina was approached by an intermediary when, after several years of trying, Foyles had failed to recover a £200 debt from an Argentinian university. Perón regretted that he could do nothing to help with this, but he sent Christina a beautifully fitted crocodile case.

J.B. Priestley (1894–1984), a loyal but not entirely uncritical friend of the management

Libya's Colonel Gadaffy deposited a satisfying £500,000 with Foyles to supply him and his government departments. 'Colonel Gadaffy is a very trustworthy client – not like some of the leaders I've dealt with,' Christina told the *Evening Standard*. Apparently the Colonel's taste embraced John le Carré, Barbara Cartland and Sherlock Holmes.

In 1994 customers in the Military Books Department were surprised to see General Augusto Pinochet purchasing a large selection of historical and military books; he complimented the department manager on the range available.

Christina's nephew, Christopher Foyle, worked at the shop from 1962 to 1972. During a Commonwealth Heads of State/Prime Ministers Conference in London, he hand-

'It is generally safe to say that if you are looking for a book "they've probably got it at Foyles".'
[The Rt Hon. The Earl Attlee]

delivered a personal letter, and with it the catalogue of an Africana section he had created, to each African leader in their hotel. The result was a visit from President Milton Obote of Uganda. 'I took him round the shop,' Christopher recalls. 'When we got to the escalator I stood aside and motioned to him to go first, but he gripped me by the arm just below the elbow and propelled me forward. I remember his intense look and extraordinarily strong vice-like grip. He was later deposed by Idi Amin.'

A year or so ago, there was comment in the UK press about the various dictators who were or had been customers of Foyles. Christopher's response – 'Dictators are people too, you know' – earned him a 'Saying of the Year' in one or two of the national dailies.

To Christopher, too, fell the pleasure of escorting the beautiful Queen Sirikit of Thailand around Foyles on her annual visit to London; he kept a discreet distance from her while she browsed with her court chamberlain and a Special Branch protection officer. When the time came to pay, the chamberlain pulled

Visitors 1960
Robert Mitchum
H. E. Bates
Nancy Spain
Wolf Mankowitz
Merle Oberon
Marty Wilde
Orson Welles
Alma Cogan
Aaron Copland
Tom Lehrer
Joyce Grenfell
Ian Fleming
Sir Malcolm Sargent
Arnold Wesker
Peter Scott
Billy Butlin

Visitors 1970

Derek Nimmo

Steve Race

Egon Ronay

Lady Antonia Fraser

Laurie Lee

Ken Dodd

Thora Hird

Dudley Moore

Daniel Barenboim

Vera Lynn

HE The Turkish

Ambassador

HE The High

Commissioner for

Mauritius

out a thick wad of new high-denomination notes and settled up in cash.

The Literary Luncheons and the book clubs brought Christina into contact with most of the great writers of her time, and the celebrities – in those days statesmen and women, intellectuals, actors and artists – who had put pen to paper. The bulk of her correspondence was with speakers and guests for the Literary Luncheons, but she wrote frequently to – among others – Dennis Wheatley, Sir Gerald Kelly and the prolific author Ethel Mannin. There are exchanges with Bernard Shaw over book-club rights to his work, with Germaine Greer about physical attacks on women; birthday greetings from John Masefield, and thanks from Earl Mountbatten of Burma for copies of *The Mountbattens* for his grandchildren. When Charlie Chaplin failed to find Winston Churchill's memoirs in Lausanne and Geneva, he turned immediately to Christina. J. B. Priestley, having a 'high opinion' of her shrewdness, sought her advice on how to persuade the public to buy *Festival at Farbridge*, 'my longest novel, my funniest...and a book that I believe hundreds of people would enjoy if only they could be enduced [sic] to read it.'

When I was working at Foyles we used to have all sorts of famous visitors. Quite frequently they would visit Christina in her old flat. On one occasion she asked me to come up to the dining room (now the Classics and Foreign Dictionary section) where I found her having a cup of tea with the enormous King Tupou IV of Tonga. He was about six foot four and twenty-five stone. He was very charming. On another occasion it was Henry Miller.

[Christopher Foyle]

'In my time I have bought every kind of book in Foyles and can't remember ever failing to obtain one, even if I have tried elsewhere in vain.'
[The Earl of Longford]

'I walked into Foyles and said, with the pomposity that students have, "I am a student of Swedish and Ancient Icelandic. I should like to know if you have a department for my subject." On the fourth floor, I was directed to a corner where I found two half-shelves, with three books on one and two on the other. The grand assistant explained, "This, madam, is our department." I said, "It's not very big." She replied, "I can assure you that this will be the biggest department for this sort of book in the world." And she was right.'
[Kate Adie]

Enid Blyton, in 1946, standing in front of a shelf of her titles

Visitors 1980
Denis Healey
Marjorie Proops
Ingrid Bergman
Susan Hampshire
Robert Lacey
Bernard Levin
Dick Francis

Visitors 1990
Claire Rayner
Richard Ingrams
Magnus Magnusson
Wilbur Smith
Jeffrey Archer
Danny La Rue
Ernie Wise
Frankie Howerd
Barbara Taylor Bradford

In response to a *Sunday Express* reader's request for the titles of twelve books published since 1900 'which every reasonably educated person should read', William chose:

English Social History, G. M. Trevelyan

The Second World War, Winston Churchill

The Old Wives' Tale, Arnold Bennett

Collected Prefaces, George Bernard Shaw

The Forsyte Saga, John Galsworthy

An Outline of History, H. G. Wells

Of Human Bondage, W. Somerset Maugham

The Good Companions, J. B. Priestley

The Wind in the Willows, Kenneth Grahame

Peter Pan, J. M. Barrie

The Story of San Michele, Axel Munthe

Gone With the Wind, Margaret Mitchell

More important than reviews or advertisements for the making of a bestseller is word-of-mouth recommendation. Best of all is praise or denunciation from a church pulpit. [William]

And the Not So Famous

Of course, not all of Foyles' customers were or are famous. People from all walks of life – students, cab-drivers, teachers, clergymen, office-workers, nuns, doctors, waiters, lawyers, police officers, artists and actors – throng its twenty-six departments. Many have written to Foyles to express gratitude for some service. *Foylibra* dutifully recorded these as 'Feather In Our Cap'.

One establishment would order old calf books from Foyles and throw them into a cupboard. When American visitors went round, they would open the cupboard and express great surprise at finding the old volumes. The Americans, thinking they must have been there for hundreds of years, would say, 'I'll give you £20 for them.' 'No,' the proprietor would say, 'I wouldn't part with them for that.' Eventually he would get about £50 and then order some more. [William]

The following three examples are typical:

- 'Thank you for the book. I had given up hope of ever getting a second-hand copy until I wrote to you. I am grateful to you for what I consider to be an excellent bargain.'
- 'I have visited Foyles on many occasions and I should like particularly to praise the competent and kindly treatment I have always received from Professor Shayan, the manager of your Oriental Languages Department.'
- 'I shall be in Britain later in the year [travelling from New Zealand] and Foyles will be one of my first ports of call.'

Sometimes the bookshop was just too efficient, as a 1954 letter from a schoolboy attests. He had written to ask whether Foyles stocked books about the Wild West, but was taken aback on his return from school to find a pile of seven on the table and a bill for £4: 'Wow! I am only fifteen years old...I have no bulging wallet like some of your customers; indeed I have no wallet.' But having fallen in love with four our young friend hit upon a plan – to scrape up the cash if Foyles would allow him a fortnight in which to pay. On his letter a pencilled note in Christina's hand says: 'Yes, will wait a month.'

Among the orders and requests that flooded in from all over the globe at least one arrived addressed to: 'Foyle's, Largest Bookshop of the World, London, England.' Enquiries ranged from books on divorce statistics to trained seals, the history of wallpaper to Stilton cheese, garbage disposal to the Morris Minor, tissue salts to T. E. Lawrence, British airports to matchbox labels, Cumbrian ballads to taxation in France, the digital microwave to British-made binoculars.

A huge number of letters in the 1950s and 1960s came from foreign students, especially in West Africa, who wrote regularly asking for free books, generally Bibles, dictionaries and atlases. Their letters were often penned in school, as a lesson, and posted in the hope that some might bring results – which, from time to time, they did.

Some customer requests were delightfully eccentric. In the 1950s, a member of the Catholic Book Club, a priest, wrote from India to say he was having a monetary exchange problem. He suggested that the club found someone to subscribe for him; in return he would say twelve masses for them during the year – 'Then I think the difficulty would be solved.' A young airman, who was taken prisoner early in 1940, wrote to say that as it seemed it would be some years before the Germans were beaten, he had decided to learn Chinese: would Foyles send him a Chinese grammar?

William and Christina were proud of, and often amused by, the letters and requests from abroad, but Christina became irritated with

Frank Harris told me he once opened a high-class restaurant in Monte Carlo. His partner was Lord Alfred Douglas. It was a failure. Harris ate all the oysters and Douglas drank all the champagne. [Christina]

demands from her wealthy home market. She noted, somewhat sourly: 'There is a certain meanness on the part of the public as regards books. Every day I receive letters from people I do not know, saying they are starting reading circles or dramatic clubs and will I give them some books. I sometimes wonder if Messrs Gamage receive letters from people saying they are starting a tennis club and will Messrs Gamage give them a gross of tennis balls, six nets and a motor lawnmower.'

She also received some curious propositions: in 1936 a request came from the USA for the address of Ben Jonson, 'to discuss film rights to *Volpone*'. An American newspaper proprietor offered £10,000 if she could get Rudolf Hess to write his autobiography – 'I believe the same gentleman offered Vincent Sheean even more in the summer of 1940 for a description of the triumphant German entry into London.'

Both she and William were keen observers of their customers – and, as the shop attracted many eccentrics, they had plenty to observe:

• A customer who came in, picked a book from the shelves, paid for it, then tore it up saying, 'I

'My wife objects to the spending of money on literature, but I need the books for my poetical works. For the sake of domestic peace, please send the books to my friend's address and I will collect them from him, without my wife knowing.' [Customer from the north of England]

hate that fellow and I always do that to his books.'

- The customer who would leave about £100 with William on Saturdays so that he would not spend it, though once William did not see him for two years.

- A man named Bell bought all books by Bell – algebra, novels and so on.

- A student, who bought a book on hanging and a few days after was found hanged with the book sticking out of his pocket.

- The man from a bank in Tottenham Court Road who spent every lunch-hour in Foyles, but never bought a book. He would bring his sandwiches, take out a new book – he was particularly fond of biography – and have a

good read. When the time came to go back to the bank, he would turn down the page and put the book back on the shelf. 'He gets very annoyed if we sell the book he is in the middle of.'

- The rabid non-smoker who used to call at the shop and argue with anyone smoking. Once, an assistant took offence and they came to blows. The police were called in.

Christina noted that the longer a customer took to choose a book the cheaper it would be. 'Even then it will often only be bought after the most searching questions about its merit and its author. Expensive books are bought quickly, while in the grip of temptation, and before sober reflection lays extravagant impulses by the heels.'

Sometimes in the general mêlée things got a bit confused. 'Once,' Christina recalled, 'after my father had locked up for the night and gone home, the telephone rang and the caller said, "I am locked in your store, but don't bother to come down tonight to get me. I'll just go back to the basement and finish picking out the books I came in for during my lunch-hour." In the morning when my father arrived the customer still had his nose contentedly buried in a book.'

On another occasion, when the lift was being repaired, Christina had a corner of the ground floor enclosed where she could interview job seekers. She saw a man waiting, invited him in and asked for his name and address. She then proceeded to interrogate him – he was thirty-five and spoke French and German. 'Why are you asking me all these questions?' he asked. 'Well,' she said, 'if you want to come to work here I have to know something about you.' He replied, 'I don't want to work here, I came in to buy a book!'

'Imagine if Kafka had gone in to the book trade.' [An exasperated customer of Foyles in the 1990s]

I once asked Conan Doyle, who became a spiritualist, if he had ever contacted literary people. Yes, he said. He had been in touch with Oscar Wilde who had passed over. Wilde said, 'Being dead is the most boring experience in the world.' [William]

In 1960 Foyles was front-page news when **Constantine Ionides** visited the shop to sign copies of his biography *Snake Man*, bringing with him three snakes. The customers crowded round him and a young clerk, who worked at **Foyles**, was bitten by the green, rat-eating snake she was stroking. She was taken to **Charing Cross** Hospital and, happily, recovered

Foyles arranged a very imposing window display for Lawrence's
The Seven Pillars of Wisdom *involving seven large papier-mâché pillars*
standing in arid-looking and appropriate sand. This display attracted a good
deal of attention; about one in three passers-by paused to examine it. The sand
in particular was greatly admired. [Bookseller]

Books Behind Bars

Some of Foyles' British customers were unable to visit the shop: a number of letters came from those detained at Her Majesty's Pleasure. An inmate of Aylesbury Prison, a member of one of the book clubs and a great reader who spent a lot on books, wrote a rather pathetic letter saying that he was anxious to qualify for the gift atlas offered to club members if they could recruit their friends. His fellow prisoners would only join if Foyles put *Gone With The Wind* in the club's selection. Christina sent him the atlas anyway, and promised to consider *Gone With the Wind*.

An inmate at Wandsworth Prison wrote in requesting a gemmologist pocket compendium and books on precious stones and hallmarks – so that he could keep his hand in. Another, at Blundeston, Lowestoft, who had a Foyles catalogue on electrical books, complained that it did not cover the one section he required: 'alarm systems and all matter and reading to do with this subject'.

Christina seems to have taken an interest in prisoners: she would record any relevant data she came across, which included the following: 'Each prisoner takes out an average of 260 books in the year. The national average for books borrowed from public libraries is only eight for each person a year.' This set her pondering: 'Does this mean that the more cultured members of the community end up in prison, or is it that the prisoner who compiled these statistics is very clever with figures?' No, she concluded: 'Life behind bars is not so urgent as in the outside world.'

Once she gave a talk at Wormwood Scrubs, where 'the questions were the most lively I have experienced'. She told the men that there was always a demand for good books and that everyone had a book in them. An inmate got up and said he had written one entitled *Five Ghastly Years*: he wanted to know how he

Before the war, the English on the whole were not a book-buying people. We in the book trade remember with horror an advertisement that depicted a woman worrying over her small boy. There he is, poring over a book, a pitiable spectacle. 'You don't want your boy to be a bookworm' ran the caption. 'You want him to be a normal healthy boy.' A few doses of Dr So-and-so's pills averted the tragedy, and you see him in the next picture chasing a football with a happy grin on his little idiot face. [Christina]

A Japanese student came in to buy a present for a retired colonel he knew, an Englishman, who was fond of something rather naughty. The student chose for the colonel What Katy Did At School, *as he thought it sounded very provocative. The colonel brought it back.*
[Christina]

should set about getting it published and what he would be likely to make out of it financially. 'I told him the procedure – literary agents, etc. – and that should a publisher accept the book he would normally be given an advance of £100. Then the book would earn royalties according to how it sold.' Another inmate immediately suggested that duplicate copies could be sent to lots of publishers thus eliciting £100 from them all. 'I explained that this was taking a very short view as he would never get another book published.'

She asked the governor of Wormwood

Most boring classics selected by hundreds of America's leading literary critics, booksellers, authors and librarians:

Bunyan's *Pilgrim's Progress*

Melville's *Moby Dick*

Milton's *Paradise Lost*

Spenser's *The Faerie Queen*

Boswell's *The Life of Samuel Johnson*

Richardson's *Pamela*

Eliot's *Silas Marner*

Scott's *Ivanhoe*

Cervantes' *Don Quixote*

Goethe's *Faust*

FOYLIBRA, JUNE 1950

Scrubs if two of his inmates could be Foyles' guests at the next Literary Luncheon for Glubb Pasha, the soldier-turned-writer Sir John Glubb. The governor was horrified, imagining questions in the House as to what two convicts were doing lunching at the Dorchester – if they got there at all and hadn't disappeared on the way. Christina told the men how sorry she was that they couldn't come. Quick as a flash, one came back: 'Please, Miss, can I come to the dinner in June? I shall be out then.'

Britain Reads Most

A recent analysis of book-reading in six major democracies, issued by the Gallup Poll, puts Britain at the top of the list and the United States at the bottom:

England	55 per cent
Norway	43 per cent
Canada	40 per cent
Australia	35 per cent
Sweden	33 per cent
USA	21 per cent

The results were based on the answers obtained to the question (books that were obviously textbooks were discounted): 'Are you now reading any books or novels?'

FOYLIBRA, MARCH 1950

Competition

A prize of one guinea is offered for the best suggestion for the quickest and most effective method of dusting Foyles' stock of over two million books. Vacuum cleaners have in the past proved unsuitable.

FOYLIBRA, JULY 1935

Foyled: "I Don't Know What Came Over Me"

Bookshop customers do not always care to pay for their purchases, and down the years Foyles has had a constant battle on its hands: shoplifters trying to outwit Foyles; Foyles trying to outwit shoplifters. The company often employed store detectives, but the family and department managers also stayed alert to the problem. Gilbert fancied himself as an amateur sleuth, though not always a successful one. Christina recalled one occasion when her uncle had become suspicious of a woman who loitered for some time. He could not keep her under observation, so asked a male customer nearby to keep an eye on her. She didn't leave and eventually the man went out. At last, Gilbert accosted her and asked what she wanted. It turned out that she was a house detective from Harrods and was keeping under observation the very man Gilbert had asked to watch her. 'Some time later, we ourselves caught this man.'

The Theology Department once phoned William to say that a suspicious character was

'How to sell a novel'

Advertisement in newspaper: 'Millionaire, young, good-looking, wishes to meet, with a view to marriage, a girl like the heroine of M—'s novel.' Within twenty-four hours the novel in question was sold out. *Montréal Star.*

FOYLIBRA

lurking there. 'Found it was my brother, Gilbert, waiting to see me.'

Christopher Foyle saw plenty of action in the late sixties and early seventies. On one occasion when he spotted a man taking books, he followed and confronted him – 'always a tricky moment as you don't know how they are going to react'. The man tried to run for it, so Christopher tackled him to the ground and a fight ensued. In the end a couple of burly policemen put an end to the fracas. It turned out that the shoplifter was an officer in MI5 who had been lifting books about code- and cipher-breaking.

Suspicions were raised by a smartly dressed middle-aged man, who often came into the shop but never bought anything. The staff soon realised what he was up to: 'We noticed that when a female customer was standing looking at books, this gentleman would be crouching down fairly close to her, apparently looking at books on a lower shelf. In reality, he had a mirror fixed to the end of a wooden stick which he would hold under the woman's skirt,' Christopher recalled.

Followed a lady up a narrow passage opposite and she took about 6 books from under her petticoat. [William]

*If you are fond of amateur detective work, then there is a
career for you here – but you must be prepared to hang
about – must be inconspicuous, very strong – sometimes
violent – a good runner – very broad-minded – merciful,
not sentimental. Must have a very wide knowledge of
human nature. What we pay: £7 or £8.*
    [Christina, notes for a speech]

The shop had some success in
apprehending thieves. In 1956 a man pleaded
guilty at Marlborough Street magistrates' court
to stealing, over thirteen years, 953 novels
valued at about £116, from bookshops in or
near London, including 344 from Foyles. On
being sentenced to three months'
imprisonment, he said: 'This has cured me of
my mania. I never wish to see a book or enter
another bookshop again.'

Occasionally Christina felt some sympathy
for the shoplifter, if not for their offence at least
for the 'marvellous ingenuity' of their excuse. A
policeman in the early hours of the morning
found a man at an open window at Foyles
busily picking up books. He assured the officer
that he had found the window open and the
books on the ground. He was replacing them in
the display. 'Alas, I was impressed less by this
expression of honest intent than by the fact of
his ten previous convictions.'

For some reason 1972 was an especially bad
year for pilfering, or perhaps Foyles and other
bookshops were particularly energetic that year
in taking offenders to court. In any event, the
newspapers were full of such stories. Students
were the most frequent culprits, tending to claim
that they needed the books for their studies. But
their teachers were not immune to temptation:
one told the court that he was 'too greedy' – the
police having found thirty-one stolen books at
his address, in addition to the four that had
landed him in court.

'This is the first time I had been to Foyles. It
was the biggest bookshop I had ever seen. I was
dazzled by the great array of books. Something I
had never seen before and which I could not
possibly get in Germany,' said a twenty-two-
year-old German student, admitting to book

thefts at Marlborough Street in 1968. He was fined fifty pounds.

'I suppose I'm a bit romantic for my age,' a fifty-three-year-old housewife told Marlborough Street magistrates' court, when she was accused of having stolen a copy of *And Yet I Love Her* and three similar novels from Foyles.

A Hemel Hempstead man, who had lived an honest life since convictions for stealing in 1946, simply couldn't resist *Climax – A Manual of Sexual Satisfaction*, on display in a branch of Martin's, the newsagent. He told Hemel Hempstead magistrates' court, 'I just don't know what came over me.'

Thomas Desmond Fenwick, a scourge of bookshops and publishers, was in and out of prison for book theft over a period of at least

Late Saturday night I caught a hefty chap stealing books. I took him round to Marlboro' St. Going along Oxford St he gave me a colossal punch on the jaw and disappeared. [William]

Often lunched with Justice Darling. Very genial and humorous. Said it is a great mistake to let book thieves off so lightly. In days of old they would be either hanged or deported. [William]

fifteen years from the mid-fifties. He had helped himself to thousands of books without paying for them, but was caught eventually, lifting a single book from Foyles, and sent down for three years. In 1966 when he was sentenced to seven years' imprisonment for fraud against publishers, the *Bookseller* reported wearily, 'So ended another instalment in the somewhat repetitious story of Fenwick's career in the book trade.'

Some imaginative scams took advantage of Foyles' second-hand business. William discovered that people would buy Bernard Shaw's plays for five shillings, ask the playwright to autograph them, then sell them back to the shop for three guineas. A youth on the staff worked out an ingenious fiddle: he took a set of children's encyclopedias from the basement and sold it to the buyer on the first floor for five pounds; he disposed of numerous school books in the same way. He was caught, but not before he had filched and disposed of a substantial amount of stock.

In another successful trick, a man went up to a cashier and said, 'I have reason to suppose that the last two five-pound notes you have taken are forgeries. I am a police officer. Would you kindly hand them to me for examination?' He said he must take the notes to the door to study them – and that was the last anyone saw of him or the notes.

After a Literary Luncheon J. B. Priestley accompanied Christina back to the shop. As he watched people browsing, he bet her that he could get away with half a dozen books. 'I went down the road and waited,' said Christina. After a few minutes, he sauntered along with an armful of books. At his heels was Foyles' store

We all knew who Silas the store detective was but took care not to blow his cover. One day we spotted him hiding behind a bookshelf, reading a book upside-down. [Former employee]

Recovered about 2000 volumes from a well-known clergyman's house; all stolen. [William]

detective. 'I just saved him from being escorted to the police station,' she said.

At least one light-fingered customer subsequently became famous. In Melvyn Bragg's biography *Rich*, the film star Richard Burton described how, when he was up at Oxford and in the RAF, he used to go to London for the weekend and steal books from 'the giant Foyles'. One day while up to his usual tricks with N, a friend, who was doing likewise, N sidled up to him casually and, out of the corner of his mouth, told Burton to 'put the books back, Taffy. Put 'em *all* back', which he did. Later, when they were safely out of the shop, N told Burton that he had seen one of the assistants go into a glass-walled office, put on a raincoat and follow him around. 'I never stole a book again,' said Burton, 'and indeed, within a year, having almost immediately become a "star", I didn't need to any more.'

In 1990 Christina received a complaint from someone who claimed they had seen two Foyles security guards beating up a man who had been caught shop-lifting. Christina promised to investigate but maintained that it couldn't have happened in Foyles. 'We don't have security guards. Possibly they were people from Waterstones or one of the many other bookshops, or maybe it was just some Soho violence, or the Mafia even...I am pretty well sure that none of our staff were involved, because people who work in bookshops are usually rather frail and avoid any kind of violence.'

Curiously, William and Christina were frequently in receipt of cash sent anonymously by repentant thieves for books they had stolen:

- £2, 'in lieu of a couple of miniature dictionaries taken without payment by a child some ten years ago who is sorry he did it'.
- £200, sent in in 1981 by a friend of someone who had 'borrowed' books some twenty years before – 'inflation has been taken into account and a contribution has been added'.
- In July 2001 Foyles received a cheque for $25 to cover three stolen books, a 'sinful' act that had troubled the sender for more than thirty years.

The caretaker lived in and one day disappeared with all the takings. Scotland Yard could not trace him. We advertised for another caretaker, offering very high salary etc. He applied for the job, giving his address. [William]

CHAPTER 5

FOYLES
LITERARY
LUNCHEONS

*'The most successful topics
are those concerned in any way
with the stage and crime.'*
[Christina]

Paul Getty (centre) with Mr and Mrs Somerset de Chair, 1961

The famous Foyles Literary Luncheons

were, of course, Christina's brainchild and bear witness to her extra-ordinary energy, confidence and chutzpah. The idea sprang from the curiosity of Foyles' customers about authors. In the late 1920s visitors to the shop told William how lucky he was that he and his family were able to meet so many writers and celebrities. Customers would come in, for example, for the latest Edgar Wallace and ask if it was true that he lived on tea and bread and butter, or whether he dictated all his books into a dictaphone.

Christina was only nineteen when she suggested that Foyles should arrange literary luncheons at which famous authors and public figures would be invited to speak. She would sell tickets to the public who wanted to see, hear and meet them. William encouraged her to go about it. She did, immediately: 'With the optimism of youth, I wrote to the five best-known authors of the day – George Bernard Shaw, H. G. Wells, Barrie, Bennett and Rudyard Kipling – suggesting a date to each of them. Of course, they all refused. Shaw said that it was hopeless to begin anything new in England. "Why not go to New York and start literary luncheons there?" he wrote. Wells, with his refusal, added a note that the letters he received from his readers convinced him that he had no desire to meet them in the flesh.'

Christina persevered and, on 21 October 1930, Foyles held its first Literary Luncheon, for two hundred people, at the Holborn Restaurant. The guest of honour was Lord Darling, a renowned judge and author, and actor/manager Sir Gerald du Maurier chaired the event. In his speech Sir

LUNCHEON NO. 22, 23 AUGUST 1932
**Sir Oswald Mosley on
'The Literature and Philosophy of Fascism':**
'Not until you have public organisation, which fascism alone can probably give, can you have anything approaching private liberty for the mass of people in this country.'

LUNCHEON NO. 45, 12 JULY 1934
Bernard Shaw on 'The Royal Society for the Protection of Birds':
'Although arrangements for the shooting of human beings on the very largest possible scale...have been brought to a perfection never achieved before, still nobody has started a society for the protection of human beings and the institution of sanctuaries where they cannot be shot...I think it is an unfortunate thing that part of the education of the governing classes of this country has always consisted of the fact that a bird was created mainly for the purpose of being shot.'

LUNCHEON NO. 51, 10 JANUARY 1935
Dr Marie Stopes on 'Dictators':
'The only way to create a happy race, a race of fine and splendid people, is to see that they are bred by mothers who are themselves free and powerful in the control of their own power of creating children – birth control, in short.'

Emperor Haile Selassie of Abyssinia arrives at the Connaught Rooms, 15 June 1936

Gerald related how on one occasion he had been summoned to serve on a jury on a day when he was due to appear in a matinée. Lord Darling was on the bench. 'I jumped up in court,' said Sir Gerald, 'and explained the position. Lord Darling asked if anyone would understudy me on the jury. Up rose the ugliest man I had ever seen in my life, and Lord Darling said, "You'll do."'

In 1931 the luncheons, about ten each year, moved to grander venues, the Grosvenor House Hotel and the Dorchester, where they soon attracted audiences of two thousand. The tradition is unbroken – except on a couple of occasions during the war years – to the present day, with the seven-hundredth on 8 May 2003.

LUNCHEON NO. 176, 25 APRIL 1946
Arthur Koestler on 'The Future of the Novel':
'The English novelist as a type has become very much the public trustee/civil-service type and that is a very great danger for the English novel, because if an art ceases to scandalise, it becomes suspect of having lost its bearing.'

LUNCHEON, 26 SEPTEMBER 1947
Enid Blyton on 'Once Upon a Time':
'...so I wrote six books under the name of Mary Pollock...They sold very well and I was very pleased, until one day I read this in a review: "Miss Enid Blyton had better look to her laurels while Mary Pollock, a new writer, is rapidly catching her up."'

LUNCHEON NO. 196, 22 APRIL 1948
Beverley Nichols on 'The New Look':
'I am quite convinced that women's figures, largely through slackness and neglect of the war years, have...very largely deteriorated...there is an immense quantity of women in London who are almost complete Qs.'

LUNCHEON NO. 223, 30 NOVEMBER 1950
Bertrand Russell on 'Celebrity':
'I have always found the best way to become a celebrity is to make enemies, because enemies will advertise your motives far more vigorously than friends.'

LUNCHEON No. 238, 2 MAY 1952
Jimmy Durante:
'I took a trip to France . . . and picked up an Italian newspaper . . . I saw in every column "Durante". So right away I got the scissors and started clipping. I must have clipped the whole newspaper, because every column had "Durante". Finally, I got someone to tell me what it was, and I found out that the word meant "during".'

LUNCHEON No. 252, 10 SEPTEMBER 1953
Randolph Churchill on Hugh Cudlipp's book
Publish and Be Damned:
'I cannot claim...to be a regular reader of the *Daily Mirror*, and frankly I do not allow the paper into my house...It seems to me that this book, masquerading as a sort of Gollancz book in bright colours, cannot be too widely read. The principles, or lack of them, by which its mammoth circulation has been brought about, are carefully explained. Crime and sex are the staple commodities which Geraldine House purveys under Mr Cudlipp's guidance to a hungry world.'

Hugh Cudlipp:
'It will come as no surprise to the people who have paid for their seats today that our Chairman has not even the courtesy to introduce the author of the "damned" book. I have torn up all my notes, unlike Mr Randolph Churchill, because I do not suffer from the inhibition which success visited upon him, which is that he is the son of a very great man.'

Christopher Foyle and Bill Samuel, Christina's nephews, have widened the scope of the Literary Luncheons with a new event: a Children's Literary Lunch. The first took place on 19 September 2002 in the Prince Albert Suite at London Zoo for year-six classes and their teachers from eight inner-London primary schools. Some twenty children's authors and illustrators shared the tables with over two hundred children, who were bursting with questions and grilled the writers on their lives, ideas, plots and characters.

Although Christina took most of the glory for the luncheons held in her lifetime, Ben Perrick, Foyles' publicity manager, became closely identified with them in the book world. To him fell the nuts-and-bolts organisation of the events, and it was he who ensured their smooth running, watchfully and unobtrusively, into his eighties.

The list of chairmen, guests of honour and speakers – several thousand – reads like a celebrity roll-call down the decades. It includes most of the great personalities from the worlds of literature, the arts, entertainment, sport, politics, law and the military, people as diverse as the Duke of Edinburgh, Harry Secombe, Michael Parkinson, Barbara Cartland, the Beatles, Bernard Shaw, Chris Bonington, Emperor Haile Selassie of Abyssinia (later Ethiopia), Anthony Eden, Harold Macmillan, Lauren Bacall, Harold Wilson, Margaret Thatcher, Donald Sinden, General Sikorski, Joan Collins, Thora Hird, General de Gaulle, John Mortimer, Bud Flanagan, Thor Heyerdahl, Lesley Garrett, Doris Lessing, Sarah, Duchess of York, T. S. Eliot, Anthony Blunt, Eleanor Roosevelt, Gloria Swanson, Edward Heath, John Mills, John Major, Field Marshal Viscount

Montgomery, Mary Quant, Peter O'Toole, Frederick Forsyth, Jane Asher, Earl Mountbatten, Jilly Cooper, Elizabeth Jane Howard, Gyles Brandreth, Edwina Currie, Lord Healey, Ned Sherrin, Victoria Wood, Terry Wogan, Bertrand Russell, Randolph Churchill, Kate Adie, Enid Blyton and Somerset Maugham.

These days the luncheons attract on average about 350 people. The paying guests come from all over the country – though the majority are from London and the Home Counties – and sometimes from abroad. Many have attended for years. Among the band of the faithful is Madame Frumkin, whom Christina invited to the first event, and Ronald Porter, who has been to more than a hundred luncheons. On the occasion of the fiftieth the regulars presented Christina with a diamond necklace.

Some frequent guests have proved a little more eccentric or unusual than others. Lady Munnings, wife of sporting painter Sir Alfred, used to bring her dog, Black Knight, with her; when he died, she had him stuffed and continued to bring him. John Haigh, the acid-bath murderer, attended until the law caught up with him.

Christina continued to pursue Bernard Shaw, who continued to put her off, with his customary twinkle: 'If I came, you would have to hire the Albert Hall'; 'If I came I should be pestered to open bazaars, swimming-baths, preside at mothers' meetings.' At last, in 1934, she persuaded him to speak about cruelty to birds – she had found that the best way to tempt a celebrity to appear at a Literary Luncheon was to ask him or her to speak on a favourite hobby, rather than on the subject for which they were famous.

LUNCHEON NO. 259, 25 JUNE 1954
Cecil Beaton on the publication of his
The Glass of Fashion:
'I was standing in Shaftesbury Avenue, trying to hail a taxi. I was wearing this suit which, as you can see, is daringly Edwardian, with its stove-pipe pants and narrow cuffs. A young man, half my age, looking as much like me as though we were two peas from the same fashionable pod, slithered up and muttered: "The job's on tonight – with razors."'

LUNCHEON NO. 293, 12 MARCH 1958
Dame Edith Sitwell on receiving the
William Foyle Poetry Prize:
'Hot water is my native element. I was in it as a baby and never seem to have got out of it since.'

LUNCHEON NO. 311, 29 JANUARY 1960
Lord Boothby on 'To Greet the Sixties':
'I think that in the sixties we shall see all this nonsense about individual powers owning atomic weapons completely changed. We shall give it up...Imagine what would happen if Castro got an atomic bomb...'

LUNCHEON NO. 326, 16 DECEMBER 1960
Barbara Cartland on the publication of the
centenary edition of Mrs Beeton's *Household*
Management:
'If you want a virile and exciting husband, you have to feed him with meat and at least two veg.'

LUNCHEON NO. 345, 20 DECEMBER 1963
David Attenborough on publication of his book *Quest Under Capricorn:*
'The most ferocious thing I have ever encountered in any trip abroad is not a snake which delivers death with one blow or even a charging rhinoceros, but the predatory immigration official.'

LUNCHEON NO. 381, 1 OCTOBER 1968
Field Marshal Viscount Montgomery of Alamein on publication of his book *A History of Warfare:*
'...It seemed to me that Man took to fighting when he became civilised, and as he became more...civilised, so wars became more and more frequent and we finally arrived today in the twentieth century when we are supposed to be very civilised, and it is the bloodiest and most turbulent century in recorded history.'

LUNCHEON NO. 418, 25 SEPTEMBER 1973
Eric Morecambe on publication of *Eric and Ernie:*
'As I look along this table, I see all these famous faces and I say to myself..."There is not one fictitious character; all the people at this table are either living or dead"...I am here to talk to you about the real author of this magnificent work, my little associate here...Is it any wonder that this man is now being hailed as the Beatrix Potter of Peterborough?'

Unfortunately she had forgotten an important detail about GBS: that, famously, he was a vegetarian. After the luncheon, Shaw strode across to his hostess: 'Protection of Birds, young lady,' he roared, 'and you give me chicken for lunch.'

Later, when she was approached by the Oxford Group, a theological group of the 1920s and 1930s, she asked Shaw if he would talk to them

Glamorous duo: Christina (right) with Eleanor Hibbert (a.k.a. Jean Plaidy), the prolific writer of romantic and historical novels, at a Luncheon in 1971

about what he thought of the movement. She enclosed a copy of the menu to show that it was vegetarian: 'One of the items was celery. I mentioned that there would be 2000 at the lunch. He said he would have come, but could not bear the thought of 2000 people eating celery.'

Other individuals were similarly, and perhaps more modestly, reticent about speaking. Lady Diana Cooper turned down the 'intolerable honour' in 1954 because she couldn't face the agony, but obliged many years later in 1981. Ian Fleming, fearful of making a fool of himself, declined in 1956, but felt able to say a few words eight years later. Violet Bonham-Carter politely refused to speak on the subject of 'A Wonderful Mother', because she felt she wouldn't be able to keep a straight face. Lucian Freud rejected Christina outright and, in no uncertain terms, told her not to ask him again.

Christina trod a fine line between forceful personalities, powerful opinion and delicate sensibilities to put together an interesting mix of guests. There were often contentious reasons for a refusal. Arnold Toynbee refused to be a guest of honour at the Literary Luncheon for Enoch Powell in 1969, and Lord Hunt thought it better if he and Mr Powell were not closely seated. Vladimir Nabokov declined an invitation to the event for Maurice Girodias as they were 'not on speaking terms'. In 1964

The Luncheons brought together celebrities from all spheres: publisher Tom Maschler, Emlyn Williams, Lauren Bacall and Lord Delfont in conversation at the Luncheon on 8 February 1974

Alistair Cooke with Douglas Fairbanks

After I had written my first book, one of the nicest things that happened to me was being invited to be a guest of honour at a Foyles Literary Lunch. That impressed me more than the sight of my own book in the shops or the sight of my own name in reviews. I was going to a Foyles Literary Lunch; I really was an author!
[Monica Dickens, 1974]

Arnold Wesker turned down an invitation to a luncheon for John Lennon (*In His Own Write*) in a lengthy, anguished letter. He felt he could not be a part of the ballyhoo surrounding the Beatles, 'a hard-working song group', whose music he found engaging as background but basically 'square'. In the event, Lennon declined to make a speech except to say, 'Thank you very much. God bless you.' Viscount Rothermere refused a luncheon on the grounds that he had already heard the cuckoo at his home in the country; there is no record of who he had been invited to listen to.

The letters of refusal were far outweighed by the expressions of appreciation from those who had spoken, though these are perhaps less interesting. Billy Graham felt that the luncheon in his honour in 1966 had been one of the highlights of his 'entire life and ministry'. Dirk Bogarde thought his birthday event one of the most moving and rewarding of his career. It was a high point, too, for Cecil B. de Mille, during a European tour. In a luncheon thank-you letter, the novelist Dorothy Eden reminded her host of advice Christina had once whispered to her, 'Get a better publisher', which she had shortly taken and not regretted. Spike Milligan, true to form, thanked her for 'your free 'ot dinner'.

Christina found she was more successful in persuading authors to appear if she called on them in person, and went to considerable trouble to do so. 'When I was nineteen, I set out to capture the well-known hotelier and sportsman, Sir Harry Preston. A journalist gave me a lift to Brighton. Sir Harry met us in the lounge of his hotel, his round face dark with anxiety. I gave him my hand. He pressed it to his heart. "Dear child," he said, "tragically the hotel is absolutely full, not a vacant room in the place. But never mind – I've made you up a little bed in my room." And for one panic-stricken moment, I believed him.'

Sir Oswald Mosley had offices near Trafalgar Square. When Christina called on him, a Blackshirt saw her up: 'Sir Oswald was looking through an enormous pile of newspaper cuttings and showed me one or two of the insulting ones. He is extremely handsome. He took me home to meet Lady Cynthia Mosley [his first wife]. She told me of her plans to launch a women's fascist movement. Luckily she died before she saw the outbreak of the terrible war, caused by fascism.'

Given the sheer number of events down the years it would be incredible to record that every show had gone smoothly. When a luncheon was held in honour of Noël Coward, to mark the publication of his autobiography, *A Talent to Amuse*, everyone was set to come – Gladys Cooper, Sybil Thorndike, Jessie Matthews, John Gielgud – except the guest of honour, who was too ill to attend. Christina remembered that Charlie Chaplin had said he would come if he was in London. In fact, he had flown especially from Switzerland to be at the celebration for Coward, who was his friend and neighbour. He arrived in England at six in the morning to find himself asked to step into the breach, which he duly did. Everyone made a tremendous fuss of him – waiters, television –

LUNCHEON NO. 442, 12 MAY 1976
The Rt Hon. Enoch Powell on publication of his book *Medicine and Politics: 1975 and After*:
'Waiting lists? Well, of course, there must be some means of reconciling infinite demand with finite resources and, if price is not going to do it, something else has to.'

LUNCHEON NO. 460, 18 MAY 1978
The Bishop of Southwark on publication of Barbara Cartland's *I Seek the Miraculous*:
'We have had a joyous friendship. It started about twenty years ago when I was sitting near her. She turned to me and said: "Honey!" I though that this was rather familiar on her part. Then I found she was merely giving me a medical prescription, from which day I have taken honey.'

LUNCHEON NO. 461, 27 JUNE 1978
Dr Rhodes Boyson, MP, on publication of his book *Centre Forward*:
'We have betrayed our young people who have been brought up with no belief in religion in many cases...no belief in patriotism, no local loyalty or family loyalty...They have moved to the worship of false gods...pop heroes and sports stars.'

LUNCHEON NO. 512, 18 OCTOBER 1983
John Mortimer, QC, on publication of *Sittings* by the Earl of Snowdon:
'I note that the only two barristers portrayed in this beautiful book are myself and Mrs Thatcher. And, as you will know, we have both given up the law to go into show business.'

Charlie Chaplin with Christina Foyle

and he admitted cheerfully that he had not missed Noël a bit.

To save time, it was Christina's practice to write and thank the speakers on the day before the luncheon; she took pride in expressing eloquent praise and appreciation for a speech she had not yet heard. On one occasion she was mortified when a typist posted the letters immediately and the speakers received them on the morning before they had spoken. But her biggest *faux-pas*, she recalled, was over the great tenor Beniamino Gigli. A friend had told her that he was in London and suggested she might persuade him to come to a luncheon.

'"Good idea," I said, and rang him up. He consented to come and speak. During the lunch, however, my friend came over and asked, "Where's Gigli?" I pointed to where the guest was sitting. "But that's not Gigli," said my friend. And it wasn't, but what could I do? I had apparently rung up the wrong person of the right name.' As it turned out, the wrong Mr Gigli made an admirable speech and no one seemed to notice.

The subjects of the luncheons have ranged from hilarious to poignant, rousing to roasting, sublime to cheerfully ridiculous. One that fell into the latter category was Reginald Reynolds's book on *Beards*. In September 1950 famous beards packed the Dorchester. Dr Josiah Oldfield, secretary of the Vegetarian Society, authors Frank Swinnerton and Arnold Haskell, the comedian Michael Bentine and the photographer Angus McBean provided, in Compton Mackenzie's words, a 'hedge of whiskers galore'. Hermione Gingold apologised for not being a bearded chairman. Despite having written comprehensively on the subject, the guest speaker did not sport facial hair. He was, he claimed, rather 'the Boswell of the Beard', but he admitted that he had once tried to grow one: his chin, he said, was 'a kind of human dust bowl in which whiskers do not thrive'.

Fascinating details were revealed about authorship. The whole of *The Scarlet Pimpernel* had come to Baroness Orczy while she was waiting for a train at Temple Underground station – 'the dreariest, dullest and most hopeless spot on God's earth'.

In 1978, at the eleventh hour, Christina landed a sought-after guest speaker in the Duke of Edinburgh. André Deutsch was publishing a book of essays on the protection of the environment. She had written to invite him to a luncheon but had heard nothing. At the last moment, the Duke said he would come. During lunch he turned to Christina: 'Do you know why I accepted? Many years ago you gave a luncheon to an old uncle of mine, Prince Christopher of Greece, when he was in exile, poor and forgotten.'

The Emperor of Abyssinia, Haile Selassie, was invited to a luncheon following his flight into exile in Britain after Mussolini's invasion of his country. The event had been arranged for some two thousand guests at the Grosvenor House when Christina realised that all the waiters were Italian. She switched it to the Connaught Rooms, where the Emperor was welcomed by a cheering crowd. During the lunch people kept sending up their menus to be signed, which Haile Selassie had expressly said he did not wish to do. William resolved the problem in characteristic fashion: he wrote on each one, 'Laugh and the world laughs with you;

LUNCHEON NO. 529, 26 JUNE 1985
Chris Bonington, fêted for his ascent of Mount Everest at the age of fifty:
'I discovered to my slight embarrassment...I had been completely flaked out when I got to the top of Everest...I was taking group pictures and everything else in a complete haze....When I got back, my wife...asked me: "Do you know what one of the members of your team was doing while you were taking all those pictures?" I looked at the transparency and there was a tell-tale jet of water going off at an angle, caught in the light of the sun.'

LUNCHEON NO. 547, 14 APRIL 1987
James Callaghan, MP, on publication of his book *Time and Chance*:
'[Harold Wilson] was usually right and I was wrong, but when I was right I could never persuade him that he was wrong.'

Luncheon No. 570, 7 February 1990
Jeffrey Bernard at a tribute luncheon for Peter O'Toole:
'It is embarrassing to find myself sitting next to our hostess, Miss Christina Foyle, because when I was sixteen...I used to steal books from her shop.'

LUNCHEON NO. 599, 15 OCTOBER 1992
Michael Parkinson, on publication of his book
Sporting Lives:
'When I was born, England had just won a test
match in Melbourne, and my father told my mother:
"We will call the boy Michael Melbourne
Parkinson." It could have been worse – we might
have won the test in Adelaide.'

LUNCHEON NO. 609, 20 OCTOBER 1993
Baroness Thatcher, on publication of her book
The Downing Street Years:
'I used to look around my cabinet and say:
"If you knew how to run industry, more of you
would be in it."'

LUNCHEON NO. 639, 13 NOVEMBER 1996
**John Major, MP, on publication of *Chequers:
The Prime Minister's Country House and Its
History* by Norma Major:**
'Whatever time I go to bed, I read for at least half
an hour. I am in the middle of reading a remarkable
work – full of double-dealing, treachery, scorn and
abuse. It is called Hansard.'

LUNCHEON NO. 643, 23 APRIL 1997
Frederick Forsyth, at his tribute luncheon:
'Years later I met another defector in
Britain...When we met and I told him my name,
he said: "Everybody in the KGB has heard of you.
The Day of the Jackal is part of the KGB
training manual."'

weep and you weep alone. Haile Selassie'. Everyone went home satisfied with their memento of the occasion.

The top table was, and continues to be, crammed with big names. There was a star-studded line-up for Sir John Gielgud in 1979: Sir Alec Guinness, Dame Anna Neagle, Anthony Shaffer, Dame Flora Robson, Sir Ralph Richardson, Carol Channing, Dorothy Tutin, Lady Diana Cooper and Edward Fox. In 1990 Denis Norden, Paul Eddington, Beryl Bainbridge, Peter Ustinov, Alan Coren, Max Jaffa, Esther Rantzen, Leslie Thomas and the High Commissioner for New Zealand were among those who turned out to celebrate Frank Muir's *Oxford Book of Humorous Prose*. Lady Thatcher's luncheon, to celebrate publication of *The Downing Street Years*, chaired by Lord Tebbit, drew Lord Hailsham, Sir Bernard Ingham, Paul Johnson, Lord Joseph, Bernard Levin, Sir David Napley, Alan Clark, Viscount Whitelaw, Lord Deedes and Sir David Frost to name but a few.

William, who only ever took the chair at luncheons for his Poetry Prize, greeted all of the guests nevertheless and reckoned to have shaken hands with about 96,000.

Apart from offering people the opportunity to see and hear authors whose work they admire, the luncheons have provided a meeting-place for everyone interested in literature and the arts, and even romance – Sandy Forsyth met her husband, Frederick, at a Literary Luncheon.

Christina took great pride in watching the concept of the event spread to other towns. The occasions gave her, too, the wonderful opportunity to observe the great and the good. She found Lawrence of Arabia shy, retiring, passionately fond of music; he would attend under the name Private

Tommy Atkins. Sir Thomas Beecham, she noted, laughed at his own jokes. Labour MP, cabinet minister and later life peer Emmanuel 'Manny' Shinwell was a frequent speaker because Christina judged him 'one of the most good-humoured, charming, modest and unassuming men I have ever met'.

She had her own ideas about anarchists, but Emma Goldman did not conform to them: 'Short, bespectacled, with the kindest of faces and the kindest of hearts, no one would believe Red Emma had been persecuted all her life. Rebecca West describes her as the most generous woman in the world, and I have met a number of people, now world famous, who owe their start in life to Red Emma. It was she who found Paul Robeson in a small southern town and was enchanted by his voice, brought him before influential impresarios and his name was made.'

Her speakers never failed to surprise her. The wittiest and often the most outspoken and lively speeches came from clergymen, while professional humourists, such as Beachcomber and P. G. Wodehouse, were often the most glum

Huw Wheldon

Barbara Cartland

Harold Wilson

Frequent speakers in their own right, Lord Tebbit and Baroness Thatcher were guests at the Seventieth Anniversary Luncheon on 18 October 2000

and pessimistic. After listening to hundreds of speakers she concluded that men were 'capable of greater wit and eloquence than women, although they are more frequently bores. Women are more sensitive to the reaction of the audience and know when they have said enough.

'From my experience, Sir Ronald Storrs, speaking on the subject of his friend, Lawrence of Arabia, gave the most brilliant speech I have ever heard. Vivien Leigh and Diana Wynyard are the most beautiful women ever to have graced our Literary Luncheons. The most successful topics are those concerned in any way with the stage and crime.'

Kate Adie, Christopher Foyle and Madame Frumkin (who attended the very first luncheon in 1930) at Luncheon No 696, 13 November 2002

The Rt Hon. Lord Jenkins of Hillhead, at a luncheon to celebrate his book *Churchill*:
'This is the first time that I have ever been given a Foyles Literary Luncheon of my own, as it were. Therefore, I regard the honour as the greater. This is far from being the first time that I have attended a Foyles luncheon or even spoken at one. Five times I have presided or made a supporting speech. Five times a bridesmaid but never before today the blushing bride. After sixteen books, I was left sixteen times, almost literally, on the shelf.'

LUNCHEON No. 691, 7 MARCH 2002
Ned Sherrin, who chaired a luncheon in honour of Joan Collins and the Rt Hon. Lord Healey of Riddlesden, included a parody of Noël Coward in his introduction:
God made trees for birds and bees
And a rib he took from Adam.
We are also aware that to make matters fair
From the spare rib he fashioned a madam.
Edna is here and deserves a big cheer,
Thank God for a plumage so steely.
For fifty-six years she has allayed all our fears
For taming the old bruiser Healey.

CHAPTER 6

THE WORLD'S GREATEST BOOKSHOP

Bookselling is a fine art. You must know when a customer is approachable and when he is not. Many book buyers dislike to be approached. It annoys them if someone pounces on them and asks them what they want, when they probably don't know themselves. [William]

The Gallery, refurbished September 2002, and used for poetry readings, launch parties and artists' workshops as well as exhibitions

FOYLED

Yes, I remember Foyles – too well –
Because, one Saturday in June,
I went to buy some books and stood
The whole confounded afternoon
In queues - to have the volumes put
Inside a paper bag and then
A stretch at the cashier's desk.
I saw that people queued again
To claim them from the foreign boy
Who served the customers or would
Have done, if he could speak the
language. No! I thought. Why ever should
I spend good money here? And left
Bookless, my education spoiled.
I would have read all Gibbon's work
By now. I tried, but I was foyled.

This poem was written as an entry for a *New Statesman*
competition in 1980. Readers were asked to contribute a poem
about waiting. Later on I learned that the magazine had asked a
lawyer to take a look at the poem, in case it was libellous. He
cleared it for publication on the grounds it was true.

WENDY COPE

Foyles Now

William Foyle was once described by an American magazine as 'The Barnum of Books' and there is still something of the 'Walk up, walk up – the Greatest Show on Earth' atmosphere about this unique shop. [Christopher Foyle]

After Christina's death,

on 8 June 1999, when management of the business passed into the hands of the family's third generation, Christopher Foyle and Bill Samuel realised that, to survive in an increasingly competitive bookselling environment, Foyles required a major overhaul. The premises needed to be refurbished, the stock refreshed and the staff revitalised, but at the same time Foyles had to retain its individuality and recover its charm. All the off-putting practices of the past – the tiresome queuing system, the hand-written chits to evidence the purchase, the absence of any stock records, the policy of not answering the telephone – had to go.

In 2002 a multi-million-pound refurbishment programme was started. Along with renovation of the building itself, including a new façade and windows, the shop is being fitted out with new shelving, lighting, flooring, lifts and air-conditioning. There has also been serious invest-ment in the latest computerised retail systems.

Foyles likes to boast the widest range of stock of any single bookshop in the United Kingdom and staff among the most highly qualified. The new management has entrusted its booksellers with further developing the stock range and encourages them to be proactive in helping customers. The ambition, shared by all, is to make Foyles, once again, the first port of call for anyone seeking specialist books and Londoners' first-choice bookshop.

But for all the change in fabric and practices the underlying ethos, of independence and individuality, remains the same. In the past two years Foyles has acquired two other retailing free spirits, which it now houses on its premises. When spiralling rents forced Europe's leading women's bookshop, Silver Moon, to close, they approached Foyles, who took over their respected name and reopened the business as Silver Moon at Foyles – a shop within a shop. A few months later Ray's Jazz – 'the first place for jazz, blues & roots and world music' and near-neighbours of the old Silver Moon – faced similar problems. They too approached Foyles – just at the time when Foyles were looking for a theme for their

I knew I was in for an interesting time when I watched the head of Accounts Payable opening the post and putting any publishers' invoices straight into the waste-paper basket! And when I asked the cashier to show me the cash book and she said, 'Which one? We have seven.' And when I found that our lecture agency, run by two septuagenarian ladies, hadn't had a booking for more than three years. [Bill Samuel in the Author]

Ray's Jazz

proposed café. The synergy was perfect and another old-established, independent business was saved. Ray's Jazz continues to stock a huge range of new and second-hand jazz recordings, CDs and vinyl, in its new home on the first floor at Foyles where it incorporates a café. As one would hope, the Café at Foyles is the complete antithesis to the homogenised chain coffee shops found in most major bookshops. It is managed by a small independent catering company which sources its ingredients from small independent producers – offering food from farms rather than factories. Foyles has often been described as a collection of specialist bookshops under a single roof. Silver Moon and Ray's Jazz add to those specialisations.

Building on the lasting popularity of the Literary Luncheons, Foyles has expanded its programme of events to include readings and signings by major authors at outside venues. These regularly attract up to a thousand people. During 2002 events were held for Nick Hornby, Michael Palin, Jeremy Paxman, Sarah Waters, Hanif Kureishi, Will Self, Donna Tartt, Maya Angelou, William Boyd and Fay Weldon among others. Smaller events are also held in the recently renovated Gallery and a long-term strategy is to develop the individuality of Foyles' many departments and create additional venues for events within the shop. This has started with reading-group meetings and author signings in Silver Moon, and live music and jazz appreciation sessions in Ray's Jazz.

In parallel with the invigoration of the bookshop Foyles has developed its own e-commerce website, which is helping rapidly to rebuild the old mail-order business from customers around the world. In the first year of operation orders were received from sixty-four different countries. Unlike pure web-based businesses, the customer service team members are all experienced booksellers, and many customers whose first contact with Foyles has been via the website go on to build a more traditional – and personal – relationship with the bookseller handling their orders. One of the first web customers sent chocolates and a photograph of himself as a young naval officer taken some sixty years earlier!

In a world increasingly dominated by multinationals and chain retailers – a world that grows ever more bland and uniform – the diversity of the book trade stands out. Even so

it is still radically different from the worlds of William and Gilbert, then Christina Foyle. Bookselling is itself dominated by chains, with the web, book clubs and supermarkets sharing much of the rest of the market. Niche markets are catered for by a great variety of small specialist shops.

Foyles enjoys the best of both worlds, stocking overall more titles than any of the mass-market outlets and with its individual departments able to compete favourably with most specialist shops. It is one of the last of the large, privately owned stockholding bookshops, with a huge range of titles covering almost every conceivable subject and catering for almost all interests. At Foyles you will find books in a remarkable number of languages, from Afrikaans to Zulu (including Bantu, Tagalog and Xhosa), taking in Basque, Brazilian Portuguese, Gulf Arabic, Tibetan, Nepalese, Serbo-Croat, Czech, Hungarian, Polish, Romanian, Estonian, Latvian, Lithuanian, Cornish, Welsh and Gaelic (both Scottish and Irish), Latin, ancient and modern Greek. You can buy *Harry Potter* in Urdu, *The Lord of the Rings* in Portuguese, Henry Miller in German, Proust in Italian, Virginia Woolf in Albanian and Omar Khayyám in English and Arabic in one volume. There is a choice of five Sanskrit and three Telugu dictionaries, and the Bible in more than twenty-five different languages.

The book trade, like so much in today's society, is a battle between the bold and the bland. The multinationals and conglomerates that dominate the book trade prefer bland for the predictability of the bottom line, concentrating on fast-selling titles to the detriment of new authors and small publishers. To maintain the diversity, and to ensure that new or non-

If you had been away from London for a few years and strolling down Charing Cross Road you saw a sign on Foyles' door that read 'Business as Usual', you would not necessarily find it reassuring…[But] it must be a treat for regular customers to find their loyalty, or long-suffering, so generously rewarded. [David Blow on the shop refurbishment, Publishing News, *July 2002]*

'…a bright and airy browser's delight, the stock is well displayed but still amazingly extensive and there's a buzzy but bookish feel about the place' [Lesley Reader, *Book Lovers' London*, 2002]

mainstream authors are made visible, requires the boldness of the independents, both publishers and bookshops. Foyles know that they can help this cause in a number of ways:

- The programme of literary events, which is widely publicised, always includes a number of non-mainstream authors.
- In-store promotions regularly feature favourite (often little-known) titles chosen by the staff.
- The twenty-one shop windows on Charing Cross Road and Manette Street are deliberately quirky, designed to stimulate interest, sometimes bring a smile and indicate to passers-by the range of books available.
- The Gallery stages an eclectic range of exhibitions: serious exhibitions, fun exhibitions, art to stimulate, art to make a point and always art to encourage book buying.

In its centenary year Foyles was voted Independent Bookshop of the Year at the prestigious British Book Awards, a wonderful accolade and reward for the efforts made by management and staff to rejuvenate this unique shop.

Main entrance on Charing Cross Road

And What of the Future?

It is a cliché, but true none the less, to say that children are our future. Foyles believes it has a key role to play in fostering a love of books in children, so the bookshop is beginning to work with local schools and the National Literacy Trust to encourage literacy. The newly renovated Children's Department, situated on the ground floor, was designed to stimulate young minds and spark their curiosity. It is arranged round a comfortable central seating area, ideally suited to storytelling events, and sports a fish tank stocked with piranhas!

Philip Ardagh, besieged at the first Children's Literary Luncheon at London Zoo, 19 September 2002

Chairman Christopher Foyle (right) and director Bill Samuel

The Foyle Foundation sponsors the Young Poets of the Year Award, which is open to children from schools throughout the UK. Foyles believes that an enraptured child may become a customer for life and that it is in the general interest of the book trade, as well as the interests of children, to encourage them to read.

In spite of regular predictions that the printed book will be rendered obsolete by later technology, book sales continue to grow. The greatest changes in the market have been in the means of delivering the book rather than in the format. The rapid development of computers and electronic communication has enabled distributors to provide efficient next-day delivery services to booksellers. Print-on-demand facilities mean that single copies of titles formerly declared 'out-of-print' can now be offered to booksellers and hence their customers. Foyles already has equipment instore to produce software CDs instantly, on demand, and monitors new trade developments closely to ensure it remains at the forefront of technological change in the twenty-first century.

A hundred years after its modest beginnings on their parents' kitchen table, William and Gilbert's enterprise is now a thoroughly modern bookshop staffed by a knowledgeable team of booksellers. It employs the latest technology and holds the widest range of book titles in the UK, plus an extensive stock of sheet music, displayed in a logical and imaginative way. It is a shop whose windows draw people into an environment that is both welcoming and stimulating. More than just a bookshop, it is a home for literary events, a place where authors enjoy meeting their readers in congenial surroundings. Above all, it is a destination, a place that is fun and interesting to visit, which customers from home and overseas consider an essential part of any visit to London – not just the UK's Independent Bookshop of the Year but perhaps, as William and Gilbert proudly boasted, The World's Greatest Bookshop.

View into the Children's Department

The British Book Awards, 24 February 2002: the Foyles team celebrate their Independent Bookshop of the Year 'Nibbie'

A couple of years ago, in a bar on a small Caribbean island with a small group of expatriate friends, an Englishman, an Irishman, an Australian and a Jamaican, I mentioned my Foyles connection. There was an immediate, respectful silence broken by the Jamaican's 'Hey, man, I didn't know you was royalty'!
[Bill Samuel in the Author]

Foyles: 113–119 Charing Cross Road, London WC2H 0EB

Open:
Monday to Saturday 9.30 – 8.00
Sunday 12.00 – 6.00

Tel: 020 7437 5660
Fax: 020 7434 1574
Email: orders@foyles.co.uk

www.foyles.co.uk

Acknowledgements

I am grateful to Christopher Foyle, Bill Samuel and members of
the family, including John Foyle, for their help and considerable
contributions and for access to the Foyle archives; in particular,
to Christopher Foyle for the history of the bookshop and family.
Thanks go also to Rita Delavigne, Derek Scott, Gloria Rouse,
Deirdre Ive and Geert-Jan Laan for their perceptive and
entertaining contributions; to Wendy Cope for allowing us to
include her poem *Foyled*; to Hazel Orme for her skilful editing;
to Ned Hoste for the elegant design; and to Vivienne Wordley
for co-ordinating the whole project. Above all, gratitude to
William and Christina, without whose eye for a good story
(sometimes embellished) this celebration of one hundred years of
their efforts would have lost a great deal in the telling.

Penny Mountain

Illustration Credits

Page 16 Dorothy Wilding, London
Page 23 & 80-81 Erich Auerbach
Page 24 Picture Service, London
Page 25 British Council
Page 26 Photo Coverage, London
Page 27 Sue Tidy
Page 32 Fox Photos
Page 37 Laurence Latimer, London
Page 38 Painting by F. E. Beresford
Page 40 John Ball
Page 44 Reproduced with kind permission of Imperial
Tobacco Ltd
Page 54 The Press Photographic Agency, London
Page 66-67 Stockwave
Page 77 and 79 Empics Sports Photo Agency
Page 102-103 Matthews News and Photo Agency,
London
Page 108 UPPA.co.uk
Page 109 Bill Bates-Van Hallan, London
Page 110 Van Hallan Photo-Features, London
Page 117 Trevor Kenyon
Page 118-119,122,123,124,125, back cover Keith Parry
Page 126 (top) Nigel Attard
Page 127 (top) Keith Parry, (bottom) Roger Tagholm

All other illustrations are from the Foyle archive at
Beeleigh Abbey.

The publisher has made every effort to contact copyright
holders. If they have been unsuccessful copyright owners
are invited to contact them directly.

'That incredible institution that only this country and city could produce – that mad, rambling, wonderful place that is changing out of all recognition, yet weirdly remains the same.'

John Simpson speaking at Foyles Literary Luncheon No 694,

September 2002